The Day They Buried Great Britain

Francis Fauquier, Lord Botetourt
and The Fate of Nations

Published by Telford Publications*

Design by 875 *Design*
Illustrations by David Eccles

© George T. Morrow II 2011

Telford Publications
301 Mill Stream Way,
Williamsburg, VA, U.S.A., 23185

Tel (757) 565-7215
Fax (757) 565-7216
e-mail: telfordpublications@msn.com
www.telfordpublications.com

FIRST EDITION

Telford Publications is named for Alexander Telford,
a volunteer rifleman from Rockbridge County, Virginia, who
served in three Revolutionary War campaigns, in the last of which,
Yorktown, he was personally recognized by Gen. George Washington
for his extraordinary marksmanship with the long rifle.

ISBN 978-0-9831468-2-7
Printed and bound by Sheridan Press, 450 Fame Avenue, Hanover, PA

The Day They Buried Great Britain

Francis Fauquier, Lord Botetourt and The Fate of Nations

George Morrow (signature)

George T. Morrow II

WILLIAMSBURG IN CHARACTER

Lord Botetourt as a young man
"A douceur enamelled on iron"

To Joan

"If a man could say nothing against a character but what he can prove, history could not be written."

SAMUEL JOHNSON

Contents

List of Illustrations

Preface

History has been obliging in juxtaposing Francis Fauquier and Norborne Berkeley, Lord Botetourt, and George Morrow makes the most of the opportunity when comparing these successive governors of Virginia, helped by their careers there being so strongly contrasted. Fauquier was a failure, a classic example of what happens when an ambassador or colonial civil servant starts taking on local colouring wherever he has been posted, and "goes native." This is close to what we, in this era of international terrorism, have learnt to call "Stockholm Syndrome," adopting the point of view of one's captors. Botetourt on the other hand was suave, patrician competence personified, a very safe pair of hands, though ones with an iron grip when necessary, easy to detect through the velvet gloves, when George Morrow draws our attention to it.

There is ample evidence that both men were steeped in the spirit of their age, the age of the European Enlightenment: preoccupied with science, with the rational approach, believing in improvement. In London Fauquier was a Fellow of the Royal Society, a member of the new Society of Arts, a governor of the fashionable charity the Foundling Hospital. In Williamsburg he was suspected of deism and had his own little circle of savants whom he entertained, including William Small who, when he returned to England, was to be responsible for introducing Boulton to Watt, making himself the matchmaker to the entrepreneurial marriage that was to give birth to the key invention of the Industrial Revolution, the rotary steam engine. As for

Botetourt, Morrow shows him nailing his Enlightenment colors to the mast when he throws out of court a reactionary and ignorant attempt to ban inoculation, the first effective weapon against smallpox.

Where the two differed was in their levels of self-assurance. On the face of it Botetourt's was boundless, while Fauquier, so clearly demonstrated here, was someone who wanted to please, needed to be liked. His father might have been deputy to Sir Isaac Newton as Master of the Royal Mint, but the suspicion must be that this was not enough to dispel a persistent feeling of social inferiority stemming from the family's refugee status as French Protestants forced to flee from the persecutions of Louis XIV. Botetourt had no such problem, born into the upper crust of county society in Gloucestershire, presumably kinsman of the mighty Gloucestershire clan of Berkeley that had been a power in the land from the early Middle Ages, his sister wife of the Duke of Beaufort, himself Colonel of the local militia, Lord Lieutenant of the County, Member of Parliament, Gentleman and then Lord of the Bedchamber at the Court of George III. What better hand could he have been dealt, more guaranteed to bolster his *amour propre* or to teach him the skills of man management that he was to display in Virginia? The only chinks in his armour were his unfortunate investments in mining, and the way he acquired his peerage in 1764.

Aristocratic involvement in the Industrial Revolution was considerable, one of the earliest and prime examples being the canal building of the Duke of Bridgewater, in order to get coal from his mines near Manchester more cheaply to market, so Botetourt was in no way exceptional when he chanced his arm in the same field. He must have gone in deep at a time when he had also been spending large sums on his house close to Bristol. The net result was that he needed to supplement his £1000 a year from his Court appointment with a salary as a colonial governor. It might have been at Madras, Calcutta or Bombay out in India, or a West Indian sugar island, or if he had been very lucky he might have landed up as Lord Lieutenant in Dublin, but as it was, he accepted Virginia gratefully. George Morrow tells us how flattered and impressed the Virginians were by his title, but they might not have been had they looked into it more closely. Unlike his foray into mining, the way he got his peerage was truly pioneering. He managed to "call it out of abeyance," that is, he found way back in his family tree an ancestor who had what was called in the Middle Ages a Barony by Writ, which could be passed down in the female line as well as the male. If the direct male line failed and more than one heiress then claimed the barony, it fell into abeyance until such time as an heiress or one of her descendants could prove that all co-heirs and their descendants were dead. Norborne Berkeley and his lawyers managed to persuade the authorities that this was the case and so, for the first time, no less than three-and-a-half centuries after it had fallen in, a Barony by Writ came out of abeyance.

In England Botetourt got little more for his pains than some, no doubt, large lawyers' bills which he could ill afford to pay, and a great deal of mockery from society, especially since he was unmarried and had no son, or daughter for that matter, to inherit the title. It was only in Virginia, where "they dearly loved a Lord" as the saying goes, that it cut any ice. Funnily enough, Lord Hillsborough, the secretary of state to whom he was answerable and with whom he crossed swords, was someone even more taken up with titles than he was. He managed to secure for himself a barony, two viscountcies, two earldoms and a marquessate, some Irish, some English, a tally only equalled later by the Duke of Wellington. But he never became what he really wanted to be, the Lord Lieutenant of

Ireland, unsurprisingly, since George III said of him, "the least man of business I ever knew."

If Botetourt suffered any suggestion of self-doubt as a result of this mockery and his financial embarrassments, it must have been dispelled by the reception he received in Williamsburg. He was soon drowning its inhabitants in a sea of his much admired "condescension," that peculiarly 18th-century quality: as George Morrow so neatly puts it, "He did not stand on his dignity, he sat on it." He was certainly much more effective in how he wielded it than was Fauquier in the way he used the word candor. The textual analysis to which Morrow subjects the contexts in which the word appears shows clearly what Fauquier was up to. He simply did not have the proconsular touch, failing to act when he should, too unsure of himself to get his timing right and so standing on his dignity, or being obsequious and hand-wringing, at quite the wrong moments. The people of Virginia played up like a horse which senses its rider is nervous, but as soon as Botetourt was in the saddle they responded to his sure, firm touch.

The irony is that a true aristocrat, Botetourt's replacement, the Earl of Dunmore, was a much worse governor than both his predecessors, though George Morrow expresses considerable doubt in his booklet on that unprepossessing Lord as to whether he can be blamed for Virginia severing herself from the mother country. Tribal, atavistic forces were abroad, both in England and in the Thirteen Colonies, and in them the Enlightenment met its match.

ROGER HUDSON

LONDON, ENGLAND

Francis Fauquier as he looked when Governor of Virginia
"Candor was a favorite word with Fauquier"

The Governor Who Loved Virginians

Lt. Gov. Francis Fauquier died on March 3, 1768. The diagnosis, known for nearly a year, was testicular cancer. There was of course no cure. Having forgone "the use of spirits, fermented liquors and animal food" and after being subjected to countless bleedings and glisters, Fauquier was eventually allowed to die in what his good friend planter Robert Carter III, standing by his bed, described as "uncommon anguish."[1]

The Governor's Bedchamber "The same bed in which his successor, Lord Botetourt, would die 31 months later"

Carter ought to have known. He visited the Governor often during those last days, and what he saw when he entered Fauquier's bedroom on the second floor of the Palace was a thin, 65-year-old man lying doubled up in pain in his bed – the same state bed, draped in the same green and white chintz and hangings in which his successor, Lord Botetourt, would die 31 months later.[2] Carter would later say of Gov. Fauquier that "his End was accompanied with uncommon Anguish, yet no Sigh or Complaint issued from his Bosom, no Pain interrupted the Serenity of his Mind" – a pattern thought by Carter to be so worthy of imitation that he advised others to "walk in his path."[3] That might be hard. The suffering experienced by Fauquier was only partly the result of disease. The rest was due to an excess of humility where it could do him least good, with his masters at the Board of Trade.[4]

Fauquier's character is expressed in his Will.[5] His gift of diamond mourning rings to his friends Robert Carter, George Wythe, William Nelson and Peyton Randolph, was as eloquent as his message was simple: they were "in remembrance of a Man who once loved them." That he was also loved in return we can be sure, if only from the character of the man revealed in his Will. To his housekeeper and cook Anne Ayscough he left £150, enough for her and her husband John, the Palace gardener, to buy and outfit a tavern on the south side of the Capitol. He was doing this, Fauquier said, "in recompense of her great fidelity and attention to me in all my Illness, and of the great economy with which she conducted the Expenses of my kitchen during my residence . . . when it was in her power to have defrauded me of several Hundred Pounds." It was meant to be a reward for Anne's honesty, but it was valued as much for what it said about his own.

The Governor's most radical act of kindness was rendered to his "poor slaves." Virginia law barred him from setting them free, but it could not stop him from offering them a degree of choice:

It is now expedient that I should dispose of my Slaves, a part of my Estate in its nature disagreeable to me, but which my situation made necessary for me; the disposal of which has constantly given me uneasiness whenever the thought has occurred to me. I hope I shall be found to have been a Merciful Master to them and that no one of them will rise up in Judgment against me in that great day when all my actions will be exposed to public view. For with what face can I expect Mercy from an offended God, if I have not myself shewn mercy to those dependent on me? But it is not sufficient that I have been their Master in my life. I must provide for them at my death by using my utmost Endeavors that they experience as little misery during their Lives as their very unhappy and pitiable condition will allow. Therefore I will that they shall have liberty to choose their own Masters, and that the Women and their children shall not be parted; that they shall have six Months allowed them to make such Choice, during which Time they shall be maintained out of my estate . . . I request it as my last Dying wish, that any person who shall retain a favorable Opinion of me, would become purchasers of such slaves [*sic*] . . . always remembering that they once belonged to me, and had been accustomed to kind Treatment which for my sake I hope they will continue to show them . . .

To ensure that his slaves were treated with humanity after his death, Fauquier in effect became his own ghost, admonishing their new owners to be kind to them because they once belonged to him. Twice in his Will, he undervalued his assets to do what was right. To give effect to his slaves' choice of master, he allowed their purchasers a 25 percent discount. To relieve the next governor of the need to take bribes to make ends meet, Fauquier offered to sell his tobacco lands to his successor for £250, a sum which, he said, was "under the real value thereof."

To allay uneasiness and avoid misunderstandings, he asked that his executors read and explain his Will to his beneficiaries, not only his wife and sons but to his slaves as well. In case any of his beneficiaries wished to dispute a bequest, he provided an inexpensive way for him or her to do it: private arbitration.

He asked nothing for his "unfeeling Carcass" except that it should be useful to science:

> [I]f it should please the Almighty God to take me off from this stage by any latent disease, with the Cause of which the Physicians or Surgeons who may attend upon me in my last Illness, may not be acquainted, my Body should be opened if they desire it, that the immediate cause of my disorder may be known, and that by those means I may become more useful to my fellow Creatures by my Death than I have been in life. I insist on this and make it part of this my last Will to take away . . . the least imputation of want of decency or respect in my dear wife or children or other Friends I may leave behind me for permitting the enquiry to be made on my unfeeling Carcass for the good of Mankind. After this examination of my Body, if necessary, I will that I be Deposited in the Earth or Sea as I shall happen to fall, without any vain Funeral Pomp and as little expence as Decency can possibly permit, Funeral Obsequies as it has long appeared to me being contrary to the Spirit of the Religion of our Blessed Saviour.

His body was not opened: his condition was too well known, his corpse too wasted by disease. Nor were most Virginians inclined in their grief to concede their Governor's habitual diffidence. In his brief but handsome memorial address to the Assembly, Council President John Blair Sr. said that the real merit and lasting legacy of Francis Fauquier was his "integrity, good sense [and] candor."[6]

Thomas Jefferson called Fauquier "the ablest man" ever to fill the job of Governor.[7] Jefferson meant it as a compliment, as of course it was, but perhaps not in the way that he intended.

Fauquier was an able man but a weak governor. He did his duty (though not always with conviction), claimed to be candid (and often was) but seemed to vacillate between excessive irritability and excessive humility.

Born in March of 1703 into a wealthy French Huguenot immigrant family from which he inherited £25,000, Fauquier was a director of the South Sea Company, a Fellow of the Royal Society, a member of the Society of Arts and a former manager and governor of the Foundling Hospital of London. He was a friend of George Frederick Handel, is said to have known William Hogarth well and is described in his proposal for membership in the Royal Society as "A Gentlemen of great merit, well versed in Philosophical & Mathematical inquiries, and a great promoter of useful Learning."[8] During his Williamsburg years he presided over a *parti carré* of amateur scientists consisting of himself, his good friend and neighbor George Wythe, William and Mary Professor of Natural Philosophy William Small, and Small's star student, the 21-year-old Thomas Jefferson. He was a great observer of scientific phenomenon – in a gentlemanly sort of way – and in 1758 sent an account of a hail storm observed in Williamsburg to be read at a meeting of the Royal Society in London.[9] He was also a fine musician, something of a religious skeptic and a gambler who was rumored to have lost his entire patrimony at the table (untrue) and "made gambling fashionable in Virginia" (only partly true).[10]

In an eulogy published in Rind's *Gazette*, Fauquier was praised for withholding "the rigour of justice [whenever it] could by any means be dispensed with" – a sort of declining balance approach to the administration of the law that exalted the ideal of doing right by doing less.[11] In fact Fauquier was not always "generous, just and mild." Like most executives, he had a temper. In matters of honor, he could be fierce. In the case of Rev. John Camm, the notoriously irritable William and Mary Professor who did everything he could to undermine Fauquier with his masters at the Board of Trade, honor seemed to require the very worst indignity that could be visited upon a Virginian.[12]

The immediate occasion for Fauquier's wrath was Camm's delivery of the King's veto of the Two Penny Act. Enacted during the great 1759 drought, the controversial Two Penny Act allowed Virginia planters to meet their obligation to pay the local clergy's salaries in cash instead of the usual tobacco, now too dear to buy at any price. The aim was to avoid unjustifiable windfalls for the clergy and potential bankruptcy for the planters. In the background of the dispute were years of conflict between the House of Burgesses and the clergy (backed by the Bishop of London) over the administration of church affairs in Virginia. Past Virginia governors had viewed the clergy as part of the establishment, as did Gov. Fauquier. The difference was that Fauquier was unwilling to leave the conduct of church business to the Church. Thus, when the rector of Bruton Parish Church failed to accede to Fauquier's request that he omit the Athanasian Creed from church services, Fauquier ostentatiously declined to rise to his feet during its reading. The point was not that he was opposed to the doctrine of one God in Trinity – Fauquier's personal beliefs remain unknown, though the local clergy seemed to think he was a deist. The point was that in his judgment the reading of the Creed was unsupported by sound reason. The devotion to logic, the questioning spirit of a man of the Enlightenment – these were central to Fauquier's character and the reason he was to find himself in continual difficulty with orthodox thinkers in both church and state.

That the King's veto was delivered "open, dirty and worn

out at the Edges and Folds"; that it was accompanied by an Additional Instruction threatening to recall Fauquier for failing to demand that the Two Penny Act include a Suspension Clause staying its effect pending approval by the King; and that the Bishop of London, speaking as head of Virginia's clergy, had called the Act "treason" – all surely contributed to turning a feud between two proud men into a transatlantic *cause célèbre*.[13] Camm's decision to bring along two clergymen, William Robinson and Thomas Warrington, to witness the delivery was another provocation. "As if," Fauquier later told the Bishop's secretary, Samuel Nicolls, "I were Villain enough to secrete or deny the receipt of my [royal] Master's Orders!"[14] As he did with most visitors, Fauquier had the three clergymen brought into the palace dining room, his daytime office. What happened next was later recounted in such detail by the participants that it can be rendered as dialogue.[15]

Camm began by telling the Governor he "had papers for him, including the order of his Majesty's Privy Council." Surprised that the Privy Council should have entrusted its orders to a mere clergyman, and a troublemaker at that, Fauquier asked, "Were these papers delivered to you open?"

"Yes, sir."

Noting that the papers were over a year old, Fauquier asked, "In whose possession have they been in all this time?"

"In mine, Sir."

"I shall write to the Board of Trade and Lords of Council to enquire about these things . . ."

"Your Honor may do as you please," replied Camm casually.

"I am well acquainted with the calumnies you have thrown on me," replied Fauquier.

"I am willing to face your Honor's informers."

"I am above board and quarrel with people to their faces," the Governor shouted, incensed that someone so "disposed to mischief" should have dared to charge *him* with using informers.

"Your Honor never quarreled with me to my face before, and I do not come to quarrel with your Honor now."

"You thought proper to visit Mr. Warrington before you waited on me."[16]

"But I escaped no better treatment from you . . ."

It was an attempt at humor – characteristically flippant, ill-timed and certainly provocative. "You are very ignorant or very impudent, take which alternative you please," the Governor replied, adding, "You are a foolish negotiator; and I order you never to enter my doors again." With that, Camm and his increasingly uncomfortable witnesses turned to leave. But Fauquier was not done. This was not the first time he had experienced Camm's impudence. "Stay!" cried the Governor. Turning to his butler Westmore, he added, "Call my Negroes; call all my Negroes!" Immediately, two black men appeared. Fauquier then called for his "Negro boy" who also came into the hall. "Here," said the Governor to his slaves, "Look at him [pointing at Camm] that you may know him again! If ever he should come to ask for me suffer him not to enter my doors!"

Writing to the Bishop of London in 1763, Rev. William Robinson described Fauquier's action as "the greatest affront that can be put upon a free man here is to give orders concerning him to the slaves, it is what a white servant would not endure with any patience."[17] What he failed to say – perhaps because it was obvious – was that Fauquier's choice of indignity said as much about his own prejudices and insecurities as it did the subject of his anger. Speaking of Camm, Fauquier wrote, "it is utterly impossible, to continue long on Terms of Amity with him or anyone influenced by or connected with him whenever he is disposed to work mischief."[18] With characteristic bluntness, Fauquier then offered the Bishop a "well meant piece of

Advice," namely that he would "direct his Commissary to break off connections" with Camm. That would not be easy. Camm was not only Rev. Robinson's good friend, he was the Bishop's. Now, thanks to his role as *ex officio* courier, he was also an emissary for the Board of Trade. Did Fauquier expect the Bishop to disavow that? And suppose it were true, as Fauquier said, that Camm and Robinson had published the story of their delivery of the King's veto with triumph? Suppose that Virginians believed, as Fauquier said, that the Board had used Camm to lessen him? How would renouncing Camm cure that? In humiliating Camm before his slaves, Fauquier had merely extended the insult, from one maddening clergyman in Williamsburg to the highest levels of the government in London – a government that since the 1688 Glorious Revolution had embraced the church as its constitutional partner.

It was highly unlikely that the Board wished to lessen any of its governors. On the other hand, Fauquier's Virginia friends were only too happy to recruit him as an ally in their increasingly bitter battle with Parliament over American rights and liberties. On the face of it, the idea of Fauquier as an ally of radicals was absurd: he might not do his duty in the first place (*vide* the Suspension Clause), but he was always at pains to do it in the second.

It was also true that the failure to allow Virginians a voice in Parliament, the amount of time that it took for letters to cross the Atlantic, and the tendency of both sides to fill up the time with rumors effectively gave the lie to every good intention and grossly exaggerated the effect of every bad one. Fauquier wanted an apology from Robinson; Robinson wished to avoid further humiliation. Had they been asked, the Board of Trade would probably have opted for silence and acquiescence. Harmony between the clergy of the established church and a royal governor was highly desirable. And if that was beyond reach, their Lordships were prepared to settle for superficial cordiality. Least desirable in the Board's view was anything that might exacerbate the dispute, and that is what they got.

According to Robinson, the Governor first broached the idea of an apology when Robinson waited on him to tell him that the Bishop had appointed him Commissary of Virginia, a position that not only guaranteed Robinson the headship of the Church in Virginia, but a seat beside the Governor as a member of the Council and a judge on the General Court.[19] Having been instructed by the Bishop to make peace with Fauquier, Robinson made a "tender of his services," begged the Governor's protection and said he was sorry if he had offended him. In return, Fauquier told Robinson he "could expect no favour from him except [he] renounced the friendship & acquaintance of Mr. Camm . . . that the memorial to the board of trade was stuffed full of d[amned] lies, that Mr. Camm had brought witnesses with him . . . that he was a clever man with a bad head & a worse heart [and] that the Bishop was a clever man but he had no better opinion of him."[20] It was a statement made, Robinson said, in "a violent rage," one that Fauquier should have immediately retracted, if only because Robinson was sure to pass it on to the Bishop as in fact he did, in quotation marks. In any case, with Fauquier in no mood for argument, Robinson chose to waive further discussion: "I assured him that I never had design'dly given him any offence & if I had any I asked his pardon." After "some time," said Robinson, Fauquier "seemed pacified & invited me to dine with him the next day."

The Governor's own recollection of this interview was that after he registered his "Observations and Remonstrances on [Robinson's] former Behaviour" he got up from his seat and took the clergyman by the hand, a gesture which he had purposely omitted until Robinson had shown that he deserved what Fauquier called this "constant Token of good will in this Country."[21] From Fauquier's point of view, the peace he "most ardently wish'd" seemed to be literally in hand. His reason for resorting to Virginia manners at this time was clear: Rev. Robinson was a Virginian.[22] Meanwhile, by speech and by gesture, Fauquier was becoming more of a Virginian himself every day.

He told Robinson that his private apology was all "any Gentleman could do, or could be asked."[23] But, as he also told the clergyman, he stood charged with "supporting the Dignity of His Majesty's Crown and the authority of his Government and on that account something more was necessary. That it was notorious to all the colony that [Robinson] had treated [him] injuriously and therefore it became necessary that the Colony should know that his Majesty's Lieutenant Governor had received reparation for his injured Honor." This was true – as far as it went. But it was also true that Fauquier's obsession with dignity was rooted in deep insecurities or, as he put it in a 1765 letter describing the near-lynching of Stamp Distributor George Mercer, "I must confess that I have never in the course of my Life been in a Situation which required so much Circumspection . . . I have often been at a loss to form a judgment for myself . . . ."[24]

Here, Robinson was willing to go the last mile for the Governor's dignity. He had not only apologized; he had done it, Fauquier admitted, "in the handsomest manner."[25] So why risk giving new offence by insisting on a second, surely less fulsome public apology? And why was it necessary to make it in front of Peyton Randolph, John Blair and Robert Carter? According to Fauquier, it was because as Attorney General and members of the Council the three men all "acted under his Majesty's sign Manual" and so were bound to "support his . . .

authority."[26] But if they were already bound to support his authority why did they need to affirm it in public? In fact, it was their first qualification that mattered most: they were all high-ranking Virginians, friends of Francis Fauquier and friends of gentlemen with whom he wished to become friends. What he called a "declaration in front of two or three friends" was a ticket to social acceptance. Here was an official who was both jealous of his official dignity and abnormally sensitive to personal slights. Here was a man for whom duty came second to emotional need; a governor who was not only too candid, but too sensitive; not only too fond of the people he governed but too reliant on their good opinion.

In short, if it was a seemingly pacified Governor who asked Robinson to dine,[27] it was an uncharacteristically solicitous, even anxious man who greeted him at the Palace door. Robinson had every reason to be surprised to find Blair, Randolph and Carter in attendance. Government officials though they might be, they were also of Fauquier's mind in matters of faith – liberals, if not skeptics on the issue of the

The Palace Dining Room
"The talk was of the fine shad"

Trinity with a long history of run-ins with the college clergy. The idea that he should apologize in front of such men was quite literally anathema to Robinson. Dinner came and went. The talk, perhaps, was of the fine shad. Fauquier then asked Robinson – presumably out the hearing of the others – "whether this was not a proper time [to apologize?]" Distressed by "a report in town & what [Fauquier] had then uttered" Robinson immediately got up and took the Governor to one side, telling him "he had much mistaken me the day before." Indeed, Robinson later told the Bishop, "there was more reason for his asking my pardon than vice versa."

"Well, well," replied the Governor.

The two men then returned to the table, but only long enough for Fauquier to announce, "I am not difficult to be pleased; whatever will satisfy these gentlemen shall satisfy me." With that, he left. According to Robinson, the others "then entered upon their parts & endeavored to persuade me [of] . . . the good [an apology] would produce – all to no avail." "And thus [Robinson concluded] the affair ended, after some altercation & one of the company's owning, that if the matter was as I said, I did all that could be expected from me. Notwithstanding this it was well propagated through the Colony that I had asked pardon of the Governor for my past conduct, in order I suppose to destroy my character, intimidate the Clergy, & shew them they were to expect no protector in me." Robinson thought he had been invited to the palace to participate in the humiliation of the church. In fact, as Fauquier suggested in his letter to Rev. Nicolls, he was there to lend consequence to the Governor.

In his letter to Nicolls, Fauquier claimed that Robinson finally yielded to reason; that when he, Fauquier, was summoned to the table, he was told that the clergyman was now ready to say that he was heartily sorry if any part of his former

behavior had given offense. It was a blanket apology, designed
to apologize for everything and thus for nothing in particular.
According to Fauquier, he then took Attorney General
Randolph aside to ask what he thought of it. "Not much" was
Randolph's response, "but for the sake of the colony he wished
peace was made," whereupon the Governor "immediately
went into the room and accepted of the recantation."[28] Even
the self-described "easy to please" Fauquier had to admit this
was not much of an apology. Indeed, he told Rev. Nicolls, it fell
"far short of what [Robinson] had given me to expect from
him." Yet, the two men shook hands and drank "to the contin-
uance of Peace and Harmony in the Colony" – a toast that
belied their true feelings and ensured that their true feelings
would haunt Church-State relations for many years to come.

That there was a connection between Fauquier's preoccupa-
tion with his dignity, the dispute over the Two Penny Act and
Fauquier's true loyalties Rev. Robinson had no doubt. When
he, Camm and the late Commissary Rev. Dawson had gone to
see the Governor about a House of Burgesses bill designed (as
Robinson put it) to "mutilate" clergy incomes, Fauquier told
them that "just or unjust, contrary to his instructions or not contrary to his instructions . . . the sole point to be considered was
how he should please the people."[29] It was not just that
Fauquier was unreceptive to their concerns; it was that he had
no sense of his duty as governor. Robinson was particularly
irked by Fauquier's continuing "zeal for the . . . [Two Penny]
Act."[30] Was the Act not highly "distressful to the Clergy?" Had
it not been disapproved by the King? And such "a humane &
pious a King" too! For Robinson, it was "an unaccountable
Mystery."[31] Quoting from what he called a "scurrilous pamph-
let [meant] . . . to abuse the Clergy & exculpate the Governor,"
Robinson noted its description of Fauquier as "incapable of
acting through mercenary motive," but only to point out that

the Assembly's recent award of £1,000 for Fauquier's "prudent conduct & unwearied assiduity in the management of public affairs" was "for certain services performed" – meaning, presumably, Fauquier's failure to give effect to the King's veto of the Act. As an offer of proof, it did not go very far; as a measure of clergy exasperation with Fauquier, it was virtually unassailable.

Ten years later, with the Revolution clearly in sight, Virginia's clergy would still be waiting for what they were owed in damages as a result of King George III's veto of the Two Penny Act – Patrick Henry having limited their reparations to one penny in the only case to be tried under the Act. It did not seem to Virginia's clergy that Francis Fauquier was a victim of slurs. Indeed, the more apologists spoke of his lack of financial motive, the more the clergy were sure of the opposite: Said Robinson, "It would never have entered . . . the head of any of the Clergy to inquire whether the Governor could possibly have any pecuniary motives . . . had the thought not been put there by . . . encomiasts."

If the clergy were puzzled by Fauquier's failure to give effect to the King's veto of the Two Penny Act, the Board of Trade was positively astonished by his failure to follow their orders and instructions. Before he left for America, Fauquier had been called before the Board and informed that the Virginia practice of combining the offices of Speaker of the House of Burgesses and Treasurer was "highly improper, liable to great inconvenience and prejudicial to his Majesty's service," and that he was to "take all . . . measures. . . to put a stop to the practice."[32] It was styled as a "recommendation" but the fact that it was transmitted at a special meeting of the Board should have told Fauquier that their lordships took the matter very seriously. In any case, a quick survey of the political landscape convinced Fauquier that it was better to let sleeping dogs lie. As he put it in a June 28 1758 letter – only his second to the Board – Speaker John "Robinson [was] the most popular man in the Country, beloved by . . .Gentlemen, and the Idol of the People."[33] In short, he very much doubted whether the Board's "recommendation" could be effected. Just three months later, he announced that he had entirely abandoned the effort, explaining that it was always impracticable during the current Speaker's lifetime and that his decision had had the good effect of giving Robinson and his friends "a great Opinion of the Openness of my Conduct."[34]

That Fauquier had traded a good opinion for a bad practice was hardly likely to satisfy the Board. When they replied on January 18, 1759, it was to reaffirm the unconstitutionality of the practice and issue a stern reprimand to him for failing to communicate with them for nearly five months.[35] If the Board was looking for action, they got it: Fauquier replied to their letter the very next day. He was "extremely chagrined"; he hoped the board "would excuse his attempts to justify himself."[36] As "[i]t was not an Instruction," he thought he "had a Latitude." Besides the Speaker was "a Man of Worth, Probity and Honor" – words that would come back to haunt him when Robinson was found to have loaned vast sums in retired currency to spendthrift planters, thereby putting the colony at risk of bankruptcy. As he often did, Fauquier interposed candor as a sort of all-purpose excuse, telling the Board he had given them "a full and candid Account," trusting in "your Lordships' Candor . . . to do the justice to acknowledge, that he apprehended bad Consequences . . . as a man of Integrity charged with the Care of his Majesties Affairs."

Candor was a favorite word with Fauquier, to be invoked defensively to spread the blame around, as when he told the Board in the same letter, " I must rely on your Lordships Candor, and beg Leave to represent to you that I was left to myself, without Instructions or Directions" or offensively, to make a virtue of a vice as when, again in the same letter, he congratulated himself for having "set the naked Truth before" the members of the Board "in a candid and undisguised Manner."[37]

The Eighteenth Century was an age of elaborate verbal courtesies. Royal governors followed suit, filling the transatlantic void to London with "humble submissions." Fauquier's letters to the Board, especially his letters of contrition, are no different in that respect. That said, if Fauquier wanted the Board to move on it was probably best that he not rely too much on lame excuses, such as "no Ship bound for London went out of these Ports for a long time" – not if he was going to also say that he had "no excuse for failing to report." Worse than his fatuous excuses were his overly-contrite admissions of wrong-doing: "I own myself very culpable; as it is undoubtedly highly improper, that any person in England should be apprised of acts of Government here, before they are communicated to your Lordships."[38] Other governors did not talk like this, or if they did, they did not subscribe themselves "impatien[t] of thinking I am in the least under your Lordship's displeasure" – not if they wished to retain the Board's respect.

The fact that there was a war on in America, the French and Indian War, and that Fauquier was busy recruiting troops for that war did cause the Board – temporarily – to get off his back.[39] But the rebukes stung and the rebuked Fauquier was even more timorous than the anxious to please, too-candid one. Nor did his mood improve when he received yet another reprimand 14 months later for assuming that his acts as Governor all required the "Advice and Consent of [his own Governor's] Council."[40] The Board dryly noted the "very dangerous and pernicious tendency" of this misapprehension. That may be one reason why Fauquier was so deeply grateful for the Board's tenderness in not reprimanding him for having (as he put it) "inadvertently fall . . . into so many errors as . . . I have done." He then went on to admit as a "Plain truth" that he had given "his assent [to three recent bills for an act, including the Two Penny Act] without ever examining" whether they had Suspension Clauses. His reason for doing this? He had received assurances from "Mr. Waller, the Clerk of General Court, an old and leading Member of the House of Burgesses" that he had "followed . . . the Custom of the House." Fauquier had simply taken Waller's word for it that the bills were "prepared according to form."[41] It was a stunning admission, probably forced from him by his desire "to take off, in a great Measure at least, the unfavorable Opinion [the Board] entertains of [my acts] at present." If so, it was made worse by his admission that he had relied on a Virginian to tell him his duty.

It was perhaps predictable that the Stamp Act years would be a time of great distress for a Governor as devoted to pleasing people as Fauquier. And in fact that proved to be the case. The near lynching of Stamp Distributor George Mercer in front of Charlton's Coffeehouse on October 30, 1765 was the culmination of months of violence, not all of it inflicted on effigies. Fauquier's report on this affair to the Board is notable for two reasons: it shows that he had warning of an impending riot; and second, it makes clear that his reason for being present at Charlton's was not to prevent the seizure of Mercer's stamps or prevent injury to him but to act as "an eye Witness of what did really did pass." Fauquier's account of this incident is a long one, but worth reading for what it says about his inability to act the part required of him:

> We were for some time, in almost daily expectations of the arrival of Colonel Mercer with the Stamps for the use of this Colony. And Rumours were industriously thrown

out, that at the Time of the General Court, Parties would come down from most parts of the Country to seize on, and destroy all Stamp'd papers. . . . These Rumours were little regarded or credited.

* * *

The mercantile people were all assembled as usual [in the Exchange, the open air area in front of Charlton's where much of the colony's import-export business was conducted]. The first word I heard was 'One and all.' Upon which as at a word agreed on before between themselves, they all quitted the place to find Colonel Mercer at his Father's Lodgings where it was known he was. This Concourse of people I should call a Mob, did I not know that it was chiefly if not altogether composed of Gentlemen of property in the Colony some of them at the Head of their Respective Counties, and the Merchants of the Country, whether English, Scotch or Virginians; for few absented themselves. They met Colonel Mercer on the way just at the Capitol. There they stop'd and demanded of him an Answer whether he would resign or

Richard Charlton's Coffeehouse
"This concourse of people I should call a mob"

act in his office as Distributor of Stamps. He said it was an
affair of great moment to him. He must consult his
Friends, and promised to give them an answer at 10 o'
Clock on Friday morning at that place. This did not satisfy them, and they followed him to the Coffeehouse, in
the porch of which I had seated myself with many of the
Council, and the Speaker who had posted himself
between the Crowd and myself. We all received him with
the greatest Marks of welcome; with which if one be
allowed to judge by their Countenances they were not
well pleased, tho' they remained quiet and were silent.
Now and then a Voice was heard from the Crowd, that
Friday was too late, the act would take place [i.e., take
effect] they would have an answer tomorrow. Several
Messages were brought to Mr. Mercer by the leading
Men of the Crowd, to whom he constantly answered he
had already given an answer and he would have no other
extorted from him. After some time, a Cry was heard 'let
us rush in' upon this we, that were at the Top of the Steps
knowing the advantage our Situation gave us to repel
those who should attempt to mount them, advanced to
the Edge of the Steps of which number I was one. I
immediately heard a Cry see the Governor take care of
him, those who were pushing up the Steps, immediately
fell back and left a small Space between me and them. If
your Lordships will not accuse me of Vanity I would say
that I believe this to be partly owing to the Respect they
bore to my Character, and partly to the Love they bore to
my person. After much entreaty of some of his Friends
Mr. Mercer was against his own Inclination prevailed
upon to promise them an Answer at the Capitol the next
Evening at five. The Crowd did not yet disperse, it was
growing dark and I did not think it safe to leave

Mr. Mercer behind me, so I again advanced to the Edge of the Steps, and said aloud I believed no man there would do me any hurt, and turned to Mr. Mercer and told him if he would walk with me through the people I believed I could conduct him safe to my house [i.e. the Governor's Palace], and we accordingly walked side by side through the thickest of the people who did not molest us; tho' there was some little murmurs. By my thus taking him under my protection I believe I saved him from being insulted at least.[42]

That Fauquier was officially obliged, as the King's Lieut-enant Governor of Virginia, to not only treat the rumors being thrown about as true but to act upon them apparently never occurred to him. He did not go to Charlton's Coffeehouse to prevent violence; he went there *to see what happened*. Mercer was on his own, and Fauquier's account of the event allowed the Board to believe that he took Mercer under his protection only because he was himself under the protection of the Speaker. Fauquier was no doubt correct in saying that his action saved Mercer from being insulted at least, and it was also true that his character was good among the Virginians. But what really impressed the mob – as Fauquier himself admitted – was the authority of the governor: "I . . . heard a Cry see the Governor take care of him, those who before were pushing up the Steps immediately fell back and left a small Space between me and them." Not until he claimed that "small space" – the space of awe, reserved for the King's appointed representative – could Fauquier say he had behaved as a governor should.

His report of the incident was not unlike his conduct at Charl-ton's that day: slow to declare itself, tentative and finally con-flicted by his dual allegiance to Virginia and to his king: "It seems to me [he told the Board] that Disorder, Confusion, and Misery are before us, unless [these] poor, unhappy deluded People in the Colonies in general should change their Plan."[43] By "plan" he meant the refusal of Virginia merchants to buy stamp taxes even for the purpose of collecting on debts. His preferred remedy, reason, had had no effect: "the flame [of revolt, he explained] had spread so universally through the colonies and every man was so heated thereby . . . no reasons could find admittance."

> I must confess that I have never in the course of my Life been in a Situation which required so much Circumspection. I have often been at a Loss to form a Judgment for myself how to proceed; and have often been dissatisfied with my determinations; and should have been glad of your Lordships superior abilities to assist me in my Conduct. If I shall be so fortunate as to have gone through this with a tolerable share of prudence, I shall think myself happy indeed.[44]

To set the "naked truth" (as he called it) before the Board, and then meekly "submit [his] conduct through the whole affair to [their lordships'] judgment" was naive. What did he want from the Board? Permission? He had that. An army? He only had to ask. As the ministry told him in their circular letter of October 24, 1765 (sent to all royal governors in America),

> If by lenient and persuasive Methods you can contribute to restore that Peace and Tranquility to the Provinces, in which their Welfare and happiness depend, you will do a most acceptable and essential Service to your Country: But having taken every Step which the utmost Prudence and Lenity can dictate, in Compassion to the folly and Ignorance of some misguided People, for the repelling all Acts of Outrage and Violence and to provide for the Maintenance of Peace and good Order in the Province, by

such time exertion of Force as the Occasion may require, for which purpose you will make the proper Application to General Gage or Lord Colville Commanders of His Majesty's Land and Naval Forces in America.[45]

London could see for itself that Americans were angry. What it could not see was why. Fauquier's inability to form a judgment – his deference to the Board's superior abilities – just passed the buck. What the Ministry wanted from its governors was crisis management: timely exertions of force *after* a trial of other methods. They got neither from Francis Fauquier – only the vague hope that he might emerge from the crisis with a reputation for prudence.

Two days after his report to the Board, Fauquier told Henry Seymour Conway that "the Dissatisfaction of the people [is] . . . too strong for my poor abilities to overcome."[46] A month later, on December 11, 1765, he told Conway the best thing he could do now was "to be patient and cool, and take no Step which would be likely to irritate the Minds of people."[47] Despite great exertions of his patience, the people were still sour nine months later – though this time it was due less to private distresses brought on by the Stamp Act than "heat and party faction . . . a Spirit of Discontent and Cavill [he said] runs throughout the Colony."[48] He was as sour as the people themselves on October 18; a month later, he was at his wit's end. Obliged to respond to the Assembly's latest provocative address, he sought to avoid "disagreeable circumstances" by replying only to the least offensive parts:

It gave me some difficulty [he told the Earl of Shelburne, the government's new American Secretary] how to frame a proper Answer, and at last have acted out of character having made much use of more art than I ever practiced with them before. But my Lord I conceived it to be the sense of his Majesty and his ministers that every disagreeable circumstance should rather be smoothed over than aggravated: therefore I picked and culled such parts of the Address as I thought would best conduce to that end; weighing every word, as I designed to say much by implication which I did not explicitly declare. Such as it is, I must submit to your Lordships' judgment, confessing at the same time I had not abilities to do better.[49]

Faced with a royal governor who preferred discretion to action, their lordships at the Board of Trade might be forgiven for failing to note the irony of the avowedly-candid Fauquier dissembling for the sake of harmony. From the Board's point of view, it was not the incautious word that was to be feared, but the Governor's excess of caution.

Inevitably, there came a time when the Governor's prudence utterly betrayed him. The British sea captain who lost his eyelashes (and much of his skin) after being tarred and feathered by a Norfolk mob for defending the Stamp Act marked a low point in Fauquier's term as governor. In a move reminiscent of Capt. Jenkins and his severed ear, over which Britain went to war with Spain in 1739, Capt. Smith first sought the assistance of Norfolk-based Capt. Jeremiah Morgan of the HMS *Hornet*. Morgan then sent Smith's letter to Fauquier in the hope that "[the Governor's] Benevolent heart will see him done Justice to."[50] Instead, Fauquier forwarded his letter to London. In view of the delicacy of the matter (the mob was led by Norfolk's mayor), he advised restraint. It was the wrong advice from the wrong man. What might seem prudent to Fauquier was sure to seem grossly inadequate to a Board grown used to timidity, self-doubt and excessively candid admissions of failure. The board had only to read Capt. Smith's letter to be "shocked," as Morgan was, by his injuries. Fauquier noted

Smith's "extreme ill usage," but only to observe that the Board could now "form a judgment of the lawless and riotous State of this colony."[51] Where was his sense of justice? Where was his sense of duty? The matter had been referred to him as Virginia's chief magistrate!

Though he declined to see justice done for Capt. Smith in April, Fauquier did not hesitate to seek the Board's help in May in arranging for his two best friends in Williamsburg – Peyton Randolph and George Wythe – to become Speaker of the House and Attorney General. "I cannot my Lords deny this truth, that I have conceived a love and esteem [for them]," he wrote. Then, sensing that "love and esteem" might need some clarification in this context, Fauquier added, "If I know my own heart, it was at first generated and has been since nourished by my observing their conduct both in public and private life, which has been uniformly void of guile, and steady in support of government." But in fact the Ministry had only to look at the enclosed list of the candidates' qualifications for office to determine Fauquier's priorities: Warm, "uniformly void of guile" himself, the Governor had put the two men's candor first on his list, loyalty to England second, just as he had put his duty to the ill-used Capt. Smith second in passing him off to the Board.

By the time testicular cancer claimed him in March of 1768, Fauquier had clearly lost his compass. Had British-American relations not been in such desperate straits, he might well have been recalled. In one way it was good that he stayed on: while he lived, affection for England lived on in Virginia. It was not so good for him, as his decision to send his wife and son Francis back to England at the end of May 1766 in anticipation of a long-promised home leave, condemned him to a lonely death.

The obituary in William Rind's *Gazette* did Fauquier the honor of a remembrance (its primary objective) and something more: It celebrated his martyrdom. What started off as a genteel, rather conventional tribute, ended as a string of apostrophes. On the basis of style alone – it is less obituary than lament – it was clearly the work of a friend. That friend was Robert Carter III, and he was addressing the people of both England and America.

In suggesting that Virginians should "walk . . . in [Fauquier's] path," Carter was not only honoring a friend he was positioning himself and his countrymen as martyrs to ignorance and injustice:

> This morning, at two o'clock, the Hon. Francis Fauquier, Esq., Lieutenant Governor and Commander in Chief of this Dominion, submitted to the relentless hand of death, and was relieved from those numerous infirmities which embittered the latter part of his existence. The many good qualities which united in this gentleman, render the tribute of reverence justly due to his memory. As a faithful representative of his sovereign, he was vigilant in government, moderate in power, exemplary in religion and merciful where the rigor of justice could by any means be dispensed with.
>
> In the exercise of his less public virtues, he was warm in his attachments, punctual in his engagements, munificent to indigence, and in his domestic connections truly paternal. Though his end was accompanied with uncommon anguish, yet no sigh or complaint issued from his bosom, no pain interrupted the serenity of his mind. His life was a pattern worthy of imitation. Let his successors there walk in his path. Let his survivors take heed to his ways. The task is not difficult, when they have before

them so strongly impressed the footsteps of this upright man.[52]

If, as Dr. Johnson would later say, a man is not upon oath where "lapidary inscriptions" (epitaphs) are concerned,[53] Carter's Fauquier was a lapidary caution for anyone unwise enough to "walk in his path." The words were from the Bible of King James. The qualities described were those of Jesus Christ. Like Christ, Fauquier had suffered cruelly, but most of his suffering was on a cross of his own making. Ostensibly an homage to a fine man, Carter's obituary supposed a man too good for this world.

Unlike Carter, Virginia's Whigs came not to lament Fauquier but to use him. In fact, the enthusiasm of one nascent rebel, the writer of a tribute to Fauquier in Rind's *Gazette* for March 10, 1768 ran so hot that his eulogy might be called a funeral pyre in prose. The idea of the Governor as a martyr equal to none, yet resigned to excruciating pain, was again emphasized – but with the twist that the Board of Trade was accused of trying to efface Virginians' love for Fauquier with repeated reprimands: "[T]his little monument [said the eulogist] is addressed by one, whose bosom retains the highest sense of those virtues possessed by that worthy Gentleman in so eminent a degree, as to make him still live in the bleeding remembrance of a numerous acquaintance, and to raise a monument in his country's bosom which is out of the power of censure to deface." Here was a British governor who was distrusted in London but loved in Virginia; here was a man who had suffered at the hands of a tyrannical government. The truth, as it so often is, was more complicated. In the years leading up to the Revolution, no one (besides Lord Dunmore) did more to sow distrust between Virginia and London than Francis Fauquier. That he tried to do right, admitted to his many inadequencies and loved Virginians, made it worse, not better.

Jefferson's praise notwithstanding, Fauquier was not an able governor, He was a popular one, but not as Lord Botetourt was popular; rather, he was popular by default – meaning, he was popular only because he failed to do his duty as a governor. When he preened himself on being on all occasions "a free-spoken man," the Board of Trade, being made up of worldly men, may have wondered whether he was being honest with them as well. When he talked about replying only to the inoffensive words in a violent Assembly address, their Lordships were invited to speculate whether he was also picking and culling from the King's Instructions. If he lost the trust of the Board – and it seems that he did – it was not because he failed to please. It was because he tried too hard, and what the Board needed was not a pleaser but an effective administrator.

Jefferson was right to suggest that Fauquier was Virginia's most learned governor, but learning, useful though it might seem to a scholar like Jefferson, is of little use to an executive, as Jefferson himself was to discover as the beleaguered governor of British-occupied Virginia. Executive office does require a degree of candor – as well as integrity, dedication and aptitude – and it is a measure of Fauquier's disability that he had all these qualities, but only in the abstract. When his dedication was put to the test, he waffled; when his integrity was fairly questioned, he became angry; and when his incompetency was exposed to view, he interposed apologies, excuses and, finally, powerlessness. Even his stand against the clergy was inspired by fear: fear that he would lose face in Virginia. If he seemed to suffer from a surfeit of moral anguish it was because moral anguish was his nature.

It is unfair to criticize Francis Fauquier for failing to avert the inevitable. He was not sent to Virginia to prevent a revolution. He was sent to carry out crown policy, something which he failed to do, while compounding his failures with admissions of failure.

Had the Board of Trade not rebuked him so early and so often, he might have been less timid. But he was not rebuked for impudence; he was rebuked for failing to do his duty as governor. That it was possible to be strong governor in the midst of a crisis, his successor would make clear. True, Fauquier was not a full governor like Lord Botetourt: nor was he a Lord of the Bedchamber. But being a lord and a governor did not prevent Botetourt being rebuked for telling the House of Burgesses exactly what he had been told to say: that the King had given his assurance there would be no new taxes on America. Nor did it stop the King from nearly sacking Botetourt's successor, the Earl of Dunmore, for threatening to make war on the colony of Pennsylvania. For all his professed love for the Virginians, Fauquier never once took their side in a dispute with the government, nor did he ever, like Botetourt, reply to a rebuke with sarcasm.

Notes

1   Robert Carter III to Benjamin Tasker, May 30, 1767, *Robert Carter Letterbooks*, Colonial Williamsburg Foundation, John D. Rockefeller Library: "Governor Fauquier hath Schirrhus Testicles [i.e., testicular cancer]. This disorder is oft mortal. He forgoes the use of spirits, fermented liquors, and animal food, (except small soup made of it). Is attended by Mr. Pope, who is an able surgeon and he tells us that the symptoms are very favorable." See also unsigned obituary of Fauquier in William Rind's *Virginia Gazette*, March 3, 1768. A comparison of the obituary with Carter's letter to his father-in-law Benjamin Tasker strongly suggests that Carter was the author of both documents.

2   Fauquier's bed was purchased from his estate by Lord Botetourt on his arrival in Virginia. It is likely that Botetourt also purchased and used Fauquier's bedcurtains. See Graham Hood, *The Governor's Palace in Williamsburg*, (Williamsburg, 1991), p. 213.

3   *Virginia Gazette* (Rind), 3 Mar. 1768.

4   See tribute by John Blair, President of the Governor's Council, to the Virginia Assembly in *Virginia Gazette* (Purdie and Dixon) 31 Mar. 1768.

5   The Will of Francis Fauquier is in the Public Record Office in London, Prob. 1/973, p. 480. Its provisions are however discussed at length in both George Reese, ed. *The Official Papers of Francis Fauquier, Lieutenant Governor of Virginia, 1758–1768*, (3 vols.; Charlottesville, Va. 1980–1983), 1: xxxvii–xxxvii, xlii–xliii and in Hood, *The Governor's Palace In Williamsburg*, pp. 143, 153, 228, 246–247.

6   *Virginia Gazette* (Purdie and Dixon), 31 Mar. 1768.

7   Thomas Jefferson, 1743–1826. *Autobiography*., Electronic Text Center, University of Virginia Library, http://etext.virginia.edu/toc/modeng/public/JefAuto.html (accessed 9/26/2010.)

8 Quoted in Reese, ed., *The Official Papers of Francis Fauquier*, 1: xxxv–xxxvi.

9 "An Account of an Extraordinary Storm of Hail in Virginia. By Francis Fauquier, Esq; Lieutenant Governor of Virginia, and F.R.S. Communicated by Williams Fauquier, Esq.; F.R.S." *Phil. Trans. of the Royal Society*, 1757, 50: 746–747; doi: 10.1098/rstl.1757.0101 (accessed 9/15/2010).

10 Reese, ed., *The Official Papers of Francis Fauquier*, 1: xl–xli. The rumor that Fauquier was a gambler comes from John Daly Burk, *The History of Virginia, From Its First Settlement to the Present Day* (4 vols.; Petersburg, Va. 1804–1816), 3:233, 333–334.

11 *Virginia Gazette* (William Rind), 3 Mar. 1768.

12 Francis Fauquier to The Board of Trade, June 30, 1760, Reese, ed., *The Official Papers of Francis Fauquier*, 1: 383. See also, Board of Trade to Francis Fauquier, 28 Nov. 1860, *ibid.*, 1: 436.

13 See Francis Fauquier to The Board of Trade, June 30, 1760, Reese, ed., *The Official Papers of Francis Fauquier*, 1: 384; "Additional Instruction," 21 Sep. 1759, Reese, ed., *The Official Papers of Francis Fauquier*, 1: 249; Bishop of London to Board of Trade, 14 Jun. 1759, William Stevens Perry, ed. *Historical Collections Relating to the American Colonial Church* (5 vols.; Hartford, 1870–1878), 1: 461–463.

14 Francis Fauquier to Samuel Nicolls, 29 July 1761, Reese ed., *The Official Papers of Francis Fauquier*, 1: 553. To quote George Reese, editor to *The Official Papers of Francis Fauquier*, "Samuel Nicolls (ca. 1713–1763) was at this time chaplain to the king, a prebend of St. Paul's, and master of the Temple, and apparently active in the business of the Society for the Propagation of the Gospel. It is not clear in what capacity he wrote [his letters] . . . but Robinson's correspondence states that he wrote . . . at the direction of the bishop of London," *Ibid.*, 1: 521. For want of a specific title, I have referred to him here as "the Bishop's secretary".

15 Francis Fauquier to Samuel Nicolls, 29 July 1761, Reese, ed., *The Official Papers of Francis Fauquier*, 1; 551–554; William Robinson to the Bishop of London, 20 Nov.1760, William Stevens Perry, ed., *Historical Collections relating to the American Colonial Church*, (1870), 1: 463–470, 464 and William Robinson to the Bishop of London, [1763?], *ibid.*, pp.472–480, 476. See also, Francis Fauquier to the Bishop of London, November 6, 1765, Reese, ed., *The Official Papers of Francis Fauquier*,

3:1298–1299 and Hood, *The Governor's Palace in Williamsburg*, p. 94, where this incident is discussed. Hood is surely correct in surmising that it began in the Palace dining room which served as the Governor's office during the day.

16   Camm's excuse for not immediately calling on the Governor upon his return to America was that he was at Rev. Warrington's house in Hampton recovering from his sea journey.

17   William Robinson to the Bishop of London, [1763?], Perry, ed., *Historical Collections relating to the American Colonial Church*, p. 476. Robinson added, "through the whole [incident] in countenance, words and gestures [Fauquier] showed himself to be in a most violent passion." *Ibid.* See also, Francis Fauquier to Richard Bland, 28 Jul. 1760, Reese, ed., *The Official Papers of Francis Fauquier*, 1: 392–393.

18   Francis Fauquier to Samuel Nicolls, 29 July 1761, Reese ed., *The Official Papers of Francis Fauquier*, 2: 551–554, 554. See also, Francis Fauquier to The Board of Trade, June 30, 1760, *ibid,*. 1: 384 (complaining of the impropriety of being sent official orders via Rev. Camm.)

19   William Robinson to the Bishop of London, 1763, (date unknown), Perry, ed., *Historical Collections relating to the American Colonial Church*, 1: 478.

20   *Ibid.* Camm's own flock – the evidently much-aggrieved parishioners of Camm's York-Hampton Parish – probably would have shared Fauquier's opinion of him, having one day looked up from their pews to find their sermon being delivered by someone they thought they had dismissed for "indecent and lascivious conduct," but who (unknown to them) had been invited back to preach by Camm in an effort at reconciliation.

21   Francis Fauquier to Samuel Nicolls, 29 July 1761, Reese, ed., *The Official Papers of Francis Fauquier*, 2: 552, 551–554. ·

22   *Ibid.* Born in Virginia and educated at Oriel College, Oxford, Robinson was also related to the Speaker of the House of Burgesses, John Robinson.

23   *Ibid.*, 2: 552.

24   Francis Fauquier to the Board of Trade, 3 Nov. 1765, Reese, ed., *The Official Papers of Francis Fauquier*, 3: 1295, 1290–1295.

25   Francis Fauquier to Samuel Nicolls, 29 July 1761, Reese, ed., *The Official Papers of Francis Fauquier*, 2: 552.

²⁶ *Ibid.* Fauquier's stated reason for insisting on a second apology from Robinson was "That it was notorious to all the Colony that he had treated me injuriously and therefore it became necessary that the Colony should know that his Majesty's Lieutenant Governor had received Reparation for his injured Honour." All very well and good. But if the injury to Fauquier was so notorious, why was he willing to take his apology in private? Fauquier's offer to "not make the affair too public," was apparently designed to make it easier on Robinson. But this still begs the essential question: How was a *private* apology in front of three men, prominent though they might be, going to repair an injury notorious to the entire Colony? The answer is clear: The apology was for Fauquier the man, whose dependence on the good opinion of his Virginia friends was a defining characteristic, both in the conduct of his office and in his relations with the Board of Trade.

²⁷ All of the quoted material on this and the following page can be found in William Robinson to the Bishop of London, [1761], Perry, ed., *Historical Collections relating to the American Colonial Church*, 1: 478–479.

²⁸ Francis Fauquier to Samuel Nicolls, 29 July 1761, Reese, ed., *The Official Papers of Francis Fauquier*, 2: 553.

²⁹ William Robinson to the Bishop of London, [1763?], Perry, ed., *Historical Collections relating to the American Colonial Church*, 1: 474.

³⁰ *Ibid.* p. 483.

³¹ *Ibid.*, p. 484.

³² Reese, ed., *The Official Papers of Francis Fauquier*, 1: 25, fn. 4 (quoting from the March 9, 1758 *Journal of the Commissioners for Trade and Plantations* (14 vols.: London, 1920–38.)

³³ Francis Fauquier to the Board of Trade, 28 Jun. 1758, Reese, ed., *The Official Papers of Francis Fauquier*, 1: 43.

³⁴ Francis Fauquier to the Board of Trade, 23 Sep. 1758, Reese, ed., *The Official Papers of Francis Fauquier*, 1: 76.

³⁵ Board of Trade to Francis Fauquier, 19 Jan. 1759, Reese, ed., *The Official Papers of Francis Fauquier*, 1: 156.

³⁶ Francis Fauquier to the Board of Trade, 10 Apr. 1759, Reese, ed., *The Official Papers of Francis Fauquier*, 1: 204–205.

³⁷ *Ibid.*

³⁸ Francis Fauquier to the Board of Trade, 3 Nov. 1765, Reese, ed., *The Official Papers of Francis Fauquier*, 3:1295.

³⁹ But *only* temporarily. On November 20, 1759 they once again

reasserted their objection to the "irregular practice" of combining the offices of Speaker and Treasurer, telling Fauquier that but for his "strong" insistence they would have immediately laid the Assembly's latest act appointing Robinson as Treasurer in front of the King for a veto. Board of Trade to Francis Fauquier, 20 Nov. 1759, Reese, ed., *The Official Papers of Francis Fauquier*, 1: 269.

40 Board of Trade to Francis Fauquier, 13 Jun. 1760, Reese, ed., *The Official Papers of Francis Fauquier*, 1: 375.

41 Francis Fauquier to the Board of Trade, 1 Sep. 1760, Reese, ed., *The Official Papers of Francis Fauquier*, 1: 403.

42 Francis Fauquier to the Board of Trade, 3 Nov. 1765, Reese, ed., *The Official Papers of Francis Fauquier*, 3: 1294.

43 *Ibid.*

44 *Ibid.*, p. 1295.

45 Henry Seymour Conway to Francis Fauquier, 24 Oct. 1765, Reese, ed., *The Official Papers of Francis Fauquier* 3: 1289–1290. Henry Seymour Conway (1721–1795) was the secretary of the Southern Department under the government that took office on 8 July 1765.

46 Francis Fauquier to Henry Seymour Conway, 5 Nov. 1765, Reese, ed., *The Official Papers of Francis Fauquier*, 3: 1297.

47 Francis Fauquier to Henry Seymour Conway, 11 Dec. 1765, Reese, ed., *The Official Papers of Francis Fauquier*, 3:1317–1318.

48 Francis Fauquier to the Board of Trade, 4 Sep. 1766, Reese, ed., *The Official Papers of Francis Fauquier*, 3 :1382–1383.

49 Francis Fauquier to the Earl of Shelburne, 18 Nov. 1766, Reese, ed., *The Official Papers of Francis Fauquier*, 3: 1394–1395.

50 Jeremiah Morgan to Francis Fauquier, 5 Apr. 1766, Reese, ed., *The Official Papers of Francis Fauquier* 3: 1349–1350, 1350; See also, William Smith to Jeremiah Morgan, 3 Apr. 1766, Reese, ed., *The Official Papers of Francis Fauquier* 3:1351–1352.

51 Francis Fauquier to the Board of Trade, 7 Apr. 1766, Reese, ed., *The Official Papers of Francis Fauquier* 3: 1352–1354. Fauquier told the Board he was also convening a meeting of the "full Council to take their Advice on what is to be done." In the meantime, he had sent Capt. Smith "to the King's Attorney," meaning Attorney General Peyton Randolph. The Captain had sought protection and deserved justice. What he got instead was an administrative runaround designed to relieve the colony's commander-in-chief and chief judicial officer,

Fauquier, of the obligation to act.

52 In another letter written at this time, Carter told Sir Jeffrey Amherst, the "full" Governor of Virginia, for whom Fauquier acted as a Lieutenant, "His burial was not pompous, for his last testament directs that that ceremony should be performed at as little expense as decency can possibly permit. He believing that the present mode of funeral obsequious [sic] was contrary to the spirit of Christ's religion." Robert Carter to Sir Jeffrey Amherst, March 9, 1768. *Robert Carter Letterbooks*, Colonial Williamsburg Foundation, John D. Rockefeller Library.

53 *Boswell's Life of Johnson*, George Birkbeck Hill ed., (6 vols; Oxford, 1934), 2:407.

The Alternative of Williamsburg

A Dawning Happiness

The Self-Executing Government of Norborne Berkeley, Lord Botetourt

Norborne Berkeley, Baron Botetourt, the second-to-last royal governor of Virginia, was that rarest of all things in colonial America: a British governor who was loved as much by the people he governed as he was by the administration in London.

Why Botetourt should be a favorite of the British Ministry is not hard to guess. He was a good Tory, a friend of King George III and the first choice of Viscount Hillsborough, the newly-appointed secretary of the government's reorganized Department of American Affairs. Among Virginians, Botetourt was to enjoy a reputation which ran the gamut from good to great. Planter Landon Carter described his brief term in office (1768–1770) as "a dawning happiness."[1] The legend on the statue of the Governor commissioned by the House of Burgesses after his death expressed its warmest gratitude for the "zeal and anxiety" Botetourt had shown in seeking to heal the "wounds and restore tranquility and happiness to th[e] whole extensive continent" of America.[2] Clearly, Norborne Berkeley would have been a hard act for any ministerial appointee to follow; for the reputed gamester, whoremaster and drunkard who succeeded him, Lord Dunmore, he was all but impossible.[3]

Whether Virginia would have revolted had Botetourt lived may be open to doubt. Whether his Lordship possessed the secret of pleasing the notoriously irritable Virginians is not. Lord Botetourt flattered their pride with his fine manners and disarmed them with his amiability, then declared that for all he could see, the government of Virginia "almost executed itself."4 The fear, expressed by Horace Walpole, that Botetourt might not "captivate" the Virginians but instead, "enrage them to a fury", was never realized; if anything, he had a deeply calming effect on them.5

That Botetourt would ultimately cause the Virginians to love him was probably as far from the American Secretary's intentions as it was remote from his powers of conjecture. The main thing, in Hillsborough's view, was that Botetourt was not Francis Fauquier, his oft–rebuked predecessor whom the Secretary suspected of too much partiality toward Virginians.6 Virtue, integrity and candor in a royal governor were fine. Diffidence and favoritism were not. And there had been hints of both in the tributes to Fauquier in the colony's two *Virginia Gazettes*.7 For Hillsborough, the course was clear: replace an unreliable, inept governor with a first-rate one.

Virginia's new non-Fauquier was to be approachable but firm; a man of character and fine manners as well as a loyal and effective leader; someone who was loyal to both king and church; in short, a paragon.

Some sense of how the people of Virginia were likely to view their new paragon is suggested by the following letter from Virginia expatriate (and former Stamp Distributor) George Mercer to his brother James, a burgess and a lawyer with an active practice before the General Court in Williamsburg. The letter suggests that George was one of the first to know of Botetourt's appointment. In fact,

Lord Hillsborough
"The main thing was that Botetourt was not Fauquier"

he may even have been consulted about it. It was the kind of case which seemed to call for counsel and George was clearly eager to provide it:

> I congratulate you and my country on the appointment of Lord Botetourt to the Government of Virginia . . . [He is] a man of a very amiable character here, remarkable for his very great attention to business, as he was said never to be absent from the House of Commons during 20 years he was member of it, at reading of Prayers or even when the House was adjourned – and he has been as remarkable since he came to the House of Peers, for his close attendance there. He never was married, has been ever recommended for his hospitality and affability, has, I believe, a very independent Fortune, and, I know, one of the prettiest seats in England, as I have often visited it with great pleasure – You'll find his Lordship's Title a very old one, though he was long kept out of it. He is one of the Lords of the King's Bed Chamber, and has always sat in the Chair, since his Title was acknowledged, when the Lords have been in a committee – upon my honor I think from his general character, and the small acquaintance I have the honor of with him, no man is more likely to make the people of Virginia happy, nor scarce anyone who will be able more and essentially to serve them here, and I do most sincerely rejoice at his appointment.[8]

Stoke Park
"One of the prettiest seats
in England"

Close attendance to the business of government was rare in 1768, and perhaps even rarer today. For Virginians, who had often complained of being neglected, Botetourt seemed a dream come true. George went on to say that he had assured his Lordship he would have James's "cheerful assistance." But if his brother wished to give the governor a recommendation for a clerk, he should remember that "his Lordship [was] a man of business, and will employ no fine proud, young Gentleman who will be above his Employment."[9]

Two months later, Lord Botetourt arrived in Hampton Roads on HMS *Rippon*. The same burgesses who had recently risked the King's displeasure by voting to increase the import duties on slaves now greeted the news of their new governor's arrival with hope and delight. But pleased though Virginians were with the governor's graces, it was his rank that really excited them. Botetourt was a Baron, a friend of the King. Unlike Fauquier, who was only a Lieutenant Governor – Governor Sir Jeffrey Amherst having followed the usual custom of appointing a surrogate while pocketing half of his salary – Botetourt was to be Virginia's first resident governor in more than sixty years.

In London, less attention was paid to Botetourt's rank than the state of his finances. Horace Walpole (who saw him a few months before he left for Virginia) told his cousin Henry Seymour Conway that Lord Botetourt was "like patience on a monument, smiling in his grief."[10] "He is totally ruined," explained Walpole, suggesting that Botetourt's decision to accept the job of Governor – at a salary of £2,000, plus emoluments – was compelled by financial necessity. Botetourt's need to leave England to avoid prosecution by his creditors was another consideration. Lord Hillsborough's calculus was surely more cynical: someone as dependent on the goodwill of the government as Botetourt could hardly afford the principled

indecision of his predecessor. For his part, Walpole saw
Botetourt as a pure instrument of the King's will, committed to
a doubtful mission to which he "[could] not be indifferent. He
must turn [the Virginians'] heads somehow," he said.[11]

Botetourt was in fact an odd combination: a smooth courtier
with muscular virtues; a risk taker with the ability to face bankruptcy with a smile; a deft political charmer with a hot temper.
Virginians would soon discover that the new governor could
keep his contradictions in balance. The business executive not
only coexisted with the fine gentleman; he gained leverage
from him – evidence, to those able to see it, that the
Gloucestershire magnate and the affable milord were one and
the same.[12]

It did not take long for the new governor to make an impress-
ion. An eight-week sea crossing in the face of strong headwinds
failed to elicit the least hint of lordly peevishness. In fact,
Botetourt had nothing but praise for the captain and crew of
HMS *Rippon*, catching people doing something right being in
his view the true spirit of noblesse oblige. "It is impossible,"
he wrote Hillsborough on October 9, "for people to live better
together than the crew of the *Rippon*."[13] The new governor was
at least as generous in describing his reactions to the Virginians
themselves. It was true that he had brushed aside an offer of
dinner from the local gentry when he first came ashore. But
anyone put off by his Lordship's "earnest request" for a chariot so that he could go at once to see "*my* Palace" was just
mean-spirited. Here was a governor willing to be pleased by
everything, from a "delightful road . . . through a forest of mag-
nificent Pines and Tulip Trees" to the "glorious Sun" above.

Near Williamsburg, Botetourt's coach was met by two members of the Governor's Council, William Nelson and his
brother, "Secretary" Thomas Nelson, who proceeded to escort

him to the capital. There he completed his conquest of Virginia, receiving congratulations and expressions of joy from the Council and rather more formal tributes of respect from city officials with equal aplomb. From the capitol, the assemblage then moved to the Raleigh Tavern's Apollo Room, there to "sup . . . at a very handsome entertainment prepared for the occasion." Botetourt did not reach his palace until ten that night. The next day, he surveyed the gardens. His impressions, detailed in an unsigned letter dictated a few days later, had little to do with the work ahead but everything to do with Botetourt himself. He wrote about "beautiful ground[s] . . . with Tulip Trees, Oaks and Pines, . . . water'd by rivulets," and about how in the spring the meadows were "cover'd with white Clover." As for relations between Britain and America, his reason for being in Virginia in the first place,

Perfect Harmony betwixt Great Britain and her Colonies

The Apollo Room
"A handsome entertainment
prepared for the occasion"

is our Constant toast. I have dissolved the House of Burgesses and am issuing Writs for a new Assembly, and if nothing happens during the first Week of their sitting, I verily think my Office will become a very pleasant Sinecure. As I flew before my family,* and have nothing as yet in order at my Palace, I dine constantly with the Principal

* That is, he left Yorktown before his servants and staff.

Gentlemen who invite me by turns; cheerfulness and plenty are always attending. And have not as yet spoiled Company.[14]

It was a charming letter; even a jovial one. What it was not was businesslike. Given the state of transatlantic affairs, given the emotional complexities of his correspondent (George III described Hillsborough as "amiable," but "the least man of business I ever knew"), this was taking a risk, even assuming that the dour Secretary's fondness for him was unfeigned.[15] Rather than promptly demand that the Assembly disclaim "erroneous and dangerous Principles" (as he was ordered to do in his Instructions), Botetourt had called for a chariot to see his palace.[16] Instead of promptly ferreting out the cause of recent "commotions", he had gone in search of a good dinner and found perfect harmony between Britain and America! As it turns out, this unsigned letter was never sent – not at least in its surviving form. Apparently, it was a draft of Botetourt's official, November 1, 1768 report to Hillsborough, which differs from the draft in that the toasts to perfect harmony were slightly less resounding, and there is an added assurance that he "[was] at present upon the best terms with all." Meanwhile the joking prediction that his post would be a sinecure had become "I like [the Virginians] stile . . . and augure well of everything that is to happen."[17]

Botetourt may have feared his humor would fall on deaf ears. But Hillsborough could not resent his show of majesty, that evocation of office which in America took the place of armies. On board the *Rippon* was a state carriage that put anything else of the sort in America to shame. At his own cost, Botetourt had restored a carriage given to him by the Duke of Cumberland, painting out the Butcher of Culloden's arms and replacing them with the Virginia shield and motto, *"En dat*

Virginia quartam," ("Behold", it now read, "Virginia supplies a fourth quarter to the world.")

That the new governor understood and exploited the power of such symbols did not go unnoticed. Forty-seven years later, he would be recalled – with unabashed nostalgia – as "a man of parade."[18] For now, he was doing exactly what Lord Hillsborough expected him to do: he was getting down to business.

Botetourt's first official act, a writ dismissing the Assembly and ordering the election of a new one, was dictated by tradition and legal necessity. What was surprising was that a man so zealously attached to the King's glory should be so quickly embraced by a people yearning for an Oliver Cromwell to stand up for America. Had Virginia's fury – so memorably voiced by Patrick Henry in 1765 – dissolved at Botetourt's approach? Or was it, as one of Botetourt's London admirers put it in a letter reprinted in the *Gazette,* that his "manly, noble and generous spirit" was simply the best "calculated to endear" him to Virginians?[19]

Time would tell. For now, the Governor's Palace was a locus of cheerfulness and plenty. At home, Botetourt served his favorite punch, made with limes purchased the week of his arrival. It helped that Williamsburg was enjoying a respite from bad news, the theater was doing comedy, smallpox was once again a bad memory and the weather (which had been cold) was suddenly warm. The main thing was that grandeur had returned to the seat of the most British of Great Britain's American colonies: "Virginia, see, thy GOVERNOR appears!" trumpeted the author of a rather artless ode in Rind's *Gazette,*[20]

> The *peaceful olive* on *his* brow *he* wears!
> Sound the shrill trumpets, beat the rattling drums
> From *Great Britannia's* isle, his LORDSHIP comes.

Bid echo from the waving *woods* arise,
And joyful acclamations reach the skies;

✦   ✦   ✦   ✦

VIRGINS
Health to our GOVERNOR,
and GOD *save the* KING –
BASS SOLO
Health to our GOVERNOR,
and GOD *save the* KING
CHORUS
Health to our GOVERNOR,
and GOD *save the* KING.

If the image of his Lordship sporting a tranquil olive on his brow verged on the grotesque, the juxtaposition of the healths to a British Governor (on page three) with the news from occupied Boston (on page two) that all was "peace and quietness, and former grievances fallen asleep" was nothing short of magical.[21]

There was even more for local Anglophiles to like in the address of the mayor and city council who complained of Botetourt having "engage[d] our affections before we . . . experienced your virtues."[22] In truth, it seemed that his Lordship came so well recommended *by himself* that formulaic tributes and fugitive testimonials from anonymous admirers were simply unnecessary. There was no denying him. From the first, Botetourt *was* his office: the amiable head of an amiable government.

Unlike Horace Walpole, Virginians never viewed Botetourt as a mere "*boncoeur*."[23] A few sour radicals may have seen him as a threat: the irrepressible agent of a repressive government. But for most Virginians, the appointment of Botetourt was a very promising sign, and at least one, Treasurer Robert Carter

Nicholas, thought his speech to the Assembly in May of 1769 actually enhanced prospects for rapprochement between Great Britain and America. As Nicholas told his friend Arthur Lee in a letter written near the end of the fall 1769 Assembly,

> after the Death of our late Governor, you Know we were extremely anxious about his Successor; . . . [but] the exceedingly amiable character given [Lord Botetourt] from every Quarter filled us with the highest Expectations of Happiness, & it is with pleasure I say it, I think his Lordship's conduct has fully justified the very high Encomiums given of him by his Friends. We were kept in Suspense till the Meeting of the late Assembly, as to what Part his Lordship would be obliged to act, with respect to our unhappy political contest [with Great Britain]: his Speech, which you no doubt will have seen before this gets to Hand, was conciliating & agreeable; we gave him, in our address, such an Answer, as showed our disposition to Peace & Quietness, reserving at the same Time, such a Latitude, as that we might not be precluded from exercising our Discretion.[24]

That Arthur Lee, the most Whiggish of four more or less radical Lee brothers*, might be persuaded to desist from detecting British plots against America by one fine speech was highly unlikely. On the other hand, Lee had always been agreeable to a redress of grievances and by year end even he had to concede Botetourt's charm, though he limited its effect to the ladies:

* Richard Henry Lee and Francis Lightfoot Lee were both signers of the Declaration of Independence, while William and Thomas Lee were more (William) or less (Thomas) ardent patriots. The eldest Lee brother, Phillip Ludwell, was a loyal member of the Governor's Council.

"Your Governor [he wrote Richard Henry Lee] is becoming very popular, as we are told here [in London] & I have the worst proof of it in the increased Orders for fineries from the Ladies at this time of general distress in their families. Either our Countrywomen are misrepresented by the Merchants Wives or they are growing deplorably extravagant."[25]

Virginians unmoved by Botetourt's graces were easily seduced by his amiability. That he was a deft practitioner of the so called "cult of sensibility" is clear from the letter below, but what strikes a modern ear as overly arch was obviously just right for an impromptu chorus of local ladies on the steps of the John Blair House:

[W]e spent a cheerfull afternoon yesterday [wrote a Williamsburg belle to her sister on August 21, 1769] – Mrs. Dawson's Family stay'd [the] Evening with us, and [the] Coach was at [the] door to carry them Home by ten o'clock but every one appearing in great Spirits it was proposed to sit at [the] steps and sing a few songs, w'ch was no sooner said than done; while thus we were employ'd, a candle and Lanthorn was observed to be coming up [the] Street (except Polly Clayton censuring their ill taste, for having a Candle such a fine Night). No one took any notice of it till we saw who ever it was stop'd to listen to our enchanting notes; Each warbler was immediately silenced: whereupon, the invader to our Melody call'd out in a most rapturous Voice, 'Charming! Charming! proceed for God's sake or I go Home directly.'

No sooner were these words uttered than all as with one consent sprang from their seats, and [the] Air echo'd with 'pray, walk in my Lord'; no indeed he would not, he would set on the Steps too, so after a few 'ha, ha, has,' and being told what all we knew, that it was a delightful evening, at his desire we strew'd the way over with Flowers, &c. &c., till a full half hour was elapsed when all retired to their respective Homes.[26]

For vivacious, twenty year-old Ann Blair, Lord Botetourt's exaggerated emphasis and little yips of joy were as disarmingly inviting as they were incontestably genuine. They were to keep singing, "for God's sake!" And if they did not? He would "go home directly!" Not all of this was verbal largesse. Nor was it the purposeful bonhomie of the born politician. Jocular threats "to leave" would become a familiar refrain in Lord Botetourt's Virginia discourse, a subtle, if constant reminder that his seemingly inexhaustible good humor had definite limits. But for Ann and her friends it was just another example of Botetourt's uncommon condescension. He did not stand on his dignity; he sat on it. So easily did he enter into the occasion, so quickly did he put everyone at ease, that it is no wonder that Horace Walpole and others thought that he was all calculation.

Botetourt was not all calculation, but neither did he ever forget his sense of duty. In England, as head of the South Gloucestershire militia, Col. Botetourt exhibited a leadership style that blended kindness and congeniality with firm discipline. He had no difficulty punishing his men for being absent from camp. But how many colonels – let alone Lords of the Bedchamber – stood sentry in place of a sergeant or a private so that they could have time off with their families? Clearly his enlisted men admired him greatly. But it was his Lordship's subaltern, Robert Jackson, divining the larger purpose in his relentless bonhomie, who took his true measure as a leader: "There is nothing that he leaves unattempted to promote the good of the Regiment, and indeed the men perform to admiration."[27] The same officer also noted Botetourt's love of the social side of camp life: his afternoon teas with the local ladies,

The John Blair House
"He did not stand on his dignity; he sat on it"

his "Assemblies, Balls, consorts, and Routs almost every night"
and "long table" dinners with the hundred and thirty-odd
scholars from Winchester College, a reflection of his lifelong
respect for learning that in Virginia was to take the form of paying for the gold medals awarded to students at the College of
William and Mary for academic excellence.[28]

Congeniality was so dear to Botetourt that he had it chiseled
in stone above the entrance to his country house at Stoke Park:
"MIHI VOBISQUE" ("For me and for you"). The desire to be
liked is very natural. Openness and approachability are fine
things in a leader. But the welcoming spirit in Botetourt was of
a different order. He was certainly no saint. In his account
books, kept by his clerk William Marshman, fees for the flog-
ging of slaves vie with alms for the poor and destitute. Whereas
Fauquier claimed to have accustomed the Palace slaves to kind
treatment,[29] Botetourt inured them to duty and hard work.
There was a limit to his kindness. He was certainly never cruel,
but he could be quite peremptory and he did expect total obe-
dience. His tart dismissal of the 1769 House of Burgesses for
asserting their sole right to impose taxes on the inhabitants of
Virginia was a case in point: "I have heard of your resolves, and

augur ill of their effect. You have made it my duty to dismiss you, and you are dissolved accordingly."[30] That a royal governor was capable of showing displeasure came as no great surprise to the burgesses. Nor were they upset to find him a zealot for the King's glory. What did surprise them, given the largely symbolic nature of their resolves, was the sudden intensity – the genuine note of shocked indignation – in his voice.

In fact, Botetourt *was* astonished by the House's abominable resolves. We know that because those were the words he actually used in his report to Hillsborough.[31] Yet his speech to the members is a model of *repressed* anger: coldly furious, intensely terse. Because he restrained the impulse to rant, his words had extraordinary impact and authority. (His unacknowledged twin, George Washington, was to do the same thing with similar results). We are told, with no effort at humor,[32] that the burgesses all left the capitol "in the greatest order." Though the full extent of Botetourt's anger was unclear to them, the burgesses had no doubt that he meant what he said.

One of Botetourt's English friends once called him "a professor of the laconic," suggesting that his terseness was studied.[33] Some of his Virginia admirers went even further. Robert Carter Nicholas' explanation for the Governor's good relations with the House was that he modeled the behavior he wanted in return: "we seem to understand each other perfectly well [Nicholas told Arthur Lee]; he . . . will do his Duty & we are determined to do what we think ours."[34] The modern view would be that clear rules, fairly and promptly applied, produce compliance. Having violated the rules, the burgesses knew what to expect, and what they expected, happened. Instead of taking offense, the burgesses were actually reassured by Botetourt's decisive manner. The contrast with the exquisitely candid Fauquier, straining to reconcile his loyalties, was audible.

For Chief Judge Botetourt, deciding a lawsuit was a chance

to affirm the rule of reason. Not content with simply deciding the case, he added dicta of his own on the wonders of modern medicine. The two defendants in the case, Norfolk Mayor Cornelius Calvert and Dr. James Dalgleish, had caused a riot in Norfolk by setting up a pest house and performing inoculations against the smallpox. The charge against them was "Maliciously intend[ing] to Spread [smallpox] all around to make a fortune."³⁵ The prosecutor, Thomson Mason, was one of Virginia's best trial lawyers, known for his love of paradox and irony. Despite that, one observer, James Parker, thought Mason had opened his case very "Simply & fully." But after that it was hard labor "in a bad Cause," with the lawyer seeking to convince the court that "cases wherein damages were Received from one who had put poison amongst his Oats, whereby Some of [his] neighbors fowls were destroyd" were somehow analogous to the crime of inciting a riot.

Sensing the court's growing impatience, Mason decided to call his first witness, one George Abyvon. Mason was hoping to show that the rioters' torching of the pest house, (which he was prosecuting in another case), was justified. He never got the chance. Botetourt was on his witness in an instant: "His Lordship asked," said Parker, "[i]f the pest house . . . was commonly occupied for that purpose & if at that time [of the inoculations] C[ornelius] C[alvert] was mayor of the Town. G Abyvon answered in the affirmative to both. 'Then,' says [Botetourt], 'the Doctr. has done his duty. Do you know,' Says he, 'any place so proper for confining that disorder as a house built for the purpose, under the inspection of the mayor & the care of a judicious physician?'" There was more testimony and no doubt, more argument, but nothing to equal the dramatic effect of Chief Judge Botetourt commandeering the prosecution's first witness. In due course, the court retired to reach a ruling.

Of the nine judges present, only John Page Jr. voted to continue the prosecution. The others – Robert Carter III, Richard Corbin, William Fairfax, John Tayloe, William Byrd III, William Nelson and John Blair, Jr. – all agreed with Botetourt that the case should be dismissed. As the parties and their attorneys were filing out of the courtroom, William Nelson decided to give vent to some second thoughts. He had acquiesced. He had done Botetourt's bidding. But now he "[e]xtend[ed] his Right arm, his face as Red as fire . . . [saying] 'If I had the power, I would hang up Every man that would inoculate even in his Own house.'" Lord Botetourt might have let this pass. He had, after all, won the day. Instead, he chose to issue a rebuke to one of the most powerful man in Virginia:

Now my friend you have given yr Opinion & very freely too, I Shall give you mine As freely . . . . The Man who first discovered Inoculation Stands unparalleled in Merit. It is the Greatest addition ever was Made to Physical Knowledge & has disarmed the most destructive foe to Mankind of all its terrors; & in a little time, the Whole World will be Convinced of this truth, Now, Sr, this is My Opinion.

Parker did not indicate whether there was a reply; but surely there was none. To the office of the court's chief justice Botetourt added the power of a governor who expected to have the last word and had had it. The hyperbole that had charmed an Ann Blair was now used to put William Nelson in his place. The piling on of superlatives ("greatest," "most," etc.), the final, brook-no-nonsense summing up, ("Now, sir, this is my opinion!") that sounded like a judgment on Nelson himself, stunned everyone. According to Parker, Botetourt then drove the point home by raising his voice so that he could be "heard

Out of Doors." Unlike his emotionally-torn predecessor, Botetourt brought moral clarity to every word he uttered. The result was admiration for him and new respect for his office – this, at a time when the people of Boston were in open revolt.

With some people, strong convictions are a leading indicator for sturdy prejudices. In Botetourt's case, they seemed to be evidence of innate good sense and fundamental decency. Thus, when James Parker visited the Palace just before the trial of Calvert and Dalgleish, he was surprised to find Botetourt willing to discuss the case, out-of-court statements by the chief judge being as improper then as they would be now. But what Botetourt wanted to discuss was not the merits of the case but the need to give both defendants and rioters "a fair opportunity" to present their evidence:

> [He] observ[ed] if the rioters had anything to advance in mitigation of their crimes they would have a fair opportunity on the trial of the indictment brought against the doctor, and at the same time it would appear whether or not we had taken due care to prevent danger. I said whatever way it was ended I should consider as right; that I hoped the people of Norfolk would be concerned that we were all bound by the same laws, and that the people they were pleased to call foreigners had as good a claim to protection and justice as if their ancestors had first settled this colony.[36]

"I would not live a day in any country where the law was partially executed," replied the Governor, deploying one of his trademark offers to leave to signal his commitment to the rule of law.[51] Given Botetourt's love of hyperbole, it was not likely that anyone would take his threat literally. Nor was Parker's willingness to accept any outcome as casual as it seemed: himself a "foreigner" (Scotsman), Parker had lost his own house in the riot, and was thus as much a victim as the defendants.

The happiness which was said to have dawned under Botetourt's rule was order.[37] Speaking of Lord Botetourt's 1769 dismissal of the House, Robert Carter Nicholas wrote that it "only purified our political air" so that the "last session . . . passed with the greatest cordiality."[38] In speaking his mind with firmness, Botetourt actually enabled dissent, even as he set limits upon it. He was probably the best judge of when *not to act* Virginia ever had, his teasing description of the colony's government as almost executing itself being the epitome of his executive style.

Whether Botetourt's enlarged views would have stood the shock of tea parties, Lexington and Concord and Patrick Henry's 1775 march on Williamsburg, is impossible to know. On October 13, 1770, just a year after exalting the merits of inoculation, the Governor was dead of a "Slight fever." It was erysipelas, not smallpox, but it was no less deadly and certainly no more treatable with 18th-Century medicines. Before he died, Lord Botetourt did admit to one regret: "'['T]is a little unluckie, had I stayd a little longer the people in America would have been Convinced, that I had their good at heart, but tis Right, whatever is is Right,' this he repeated twice or thrice."[39]

His funeral was perhaps the grandest – and saddest

Lord Botetourt's funeral, as interpreted by Colonial Williamsburg "The grandest – and saddest – ever held in Williamsburg"

– ever held in Williamsburg. At one o'clock on Friday afternoon, October 19, 1770, all the bells in Williamsburg began to toll. Precisely at two, those who had received an invitation to follow Botetourt's corpse to its place of interment in the chapel of the College of William and Mary gathered at the Governor's Palace. At three o'clock, the coffin was placed on the hearse and the cortege, passing through a corridor of militia, moved down Palace Street to Bruton Parish Church for the reading of the funeral service.

It was all done with strict attention to rank and decorum as befit the man and the sadness of the day. If the notice in the *Gazette* sounded epochal it was not only because solemn words and high ritual were part of the event, but because the event was felt by many Virginians to mark the passing of an age:[40]

The HEARSE

Preceded by two mutes*, and three on each side the hearse,
Outward of whom walked the pall bearers,
Composed of six of his Majesty's Council,
And the Hon. the Speaker, and Richard Bland, Esq;
of the House of Burgesses.
His Excellency's servants, in deep mourning.
The Gentlemen of the Clergy, and
Professors of the College.
Clerk of the Church, and Organist.
Immediately followed the hearse the Chief Mourners
Gentlemen of the Faculty.
Mayor, Recorder, Aldermen, and
Common Council of the city,
With the mace born before them.
Gentlemen of the Law, and Clerk of the General Court,

---

* A Roman custom. A symbolic protector of the deceased, the mute's main purpose at a funeral was to look sad and pathetic.

Ushers, Students, and Scholars of
William and Mary college,
All having white hatbands and gloves,
And then the company, which was very numerous,
Two and two.

When the procession reached the church's west entrance an
honor guard of gentlemen carried the coffin to the center of the
church and placed it on a black carpet. The attendees took
their seats, all according to rank. The vicar, Rev. Mr. Woolls,
then led them in an anthem with Peter Pelham, Bruton
Parish's organist (and Botetourt's part-time clerk), at the organ.
The Commissary, Mr. Horrocks, delivered the sermon. It was
from Psalm xlii, *Put thy trust in God*, which, "joined to the deep
affliction felt by the whole audience," seemed to draw tears
from many. The coffin, said to be made "of lead, with a cover
of crimson velvet, adorned with silver handles," was then
replaced on the hearse and taken to William and Mary for burial under Botetourt's favorite pew.[41]

On October 30, William Nelson wrote to the Duke of Beaufort, informing him of the sad fact of his uncle's death, the
grandeur of his funeral ("attended with some
expence") and the colony's intentions with
respect to assembling and disposing of Botetourt's Virginia estate.[42] The letter, with its
attached inventory of Botetourt's effects,
reached Badminton on New Year's Day. The
Duke replied at once, complimenting Nelson
for "directing so very handsome a funeral and
conducting it with so much Order and
Decency." He also offered to pay any
expense incurred. Nelson's proposal for the
disposition of Lord Botetourt's things was

Henry Somerset,
Duke of Beaufort
"The dignity was
hard won"

entirely acceptable to the Duke. He asked only that he be permitted to erect a monument to his "dear uncle" in the college chapel. As for Botetourt's state coach and the paintings of the King and Queen he had brought with him to Virginia, the Duke hoped that the colony would accept them as a small return for the many marks of esteem they had shown to Botetourt when he was ill, and for the "Regard . . . paid to his Memory, in his funeral."[43]

The Duke's request that he might be allowed to erect a monument to Botetourt was laid before the Virginia General Assembly by William Nelson at its July 1771 session. The burgesses liked the idea; liked it so well that they voted to fund a statue at public expense. "We should . . . think ourselves wanting in . . . Regard . . . to our Country," they declared, "did we not seize this first Opportunity of publicly paying a just tribute to so high a character." Nelson was instructed to procure "an elegant Statue of his late Excellency . . . in Marble . . . with proper inscriptions."[44]

The statue, by English sculptor Richard Hayward, arrived in Virginia in mid-1773. It cost nearly £1,000, a rather large sum for a colony still teetering on the edge of bankruptcy. Col. Richard Bland, whose 1765 essay attacking the constitutionality of the Stamp Act would later be viewed as the first literary shot of the rebellion, composed the inscription:

AMERICA, BEHOLD YOUR FRIEND WHO LEAVING HIS NATIVE COUNTRY DECLINED THOSE ADDITIONAL HONOURS WHICH WERE THERE IN STORE FOR HIM THAT HE MIGHT HEAL YOUR WOUNDS AND RESTORE TRANQUILITY AND HAPPINESS TO THIS EXTENSIVE CONTINENT; WITH WHAT ZEAL AND ANXIETY HE PURSUED THESE GLORIOUS OBJECTS, VIRGINIA, THUS BEARS HER GRATEFULL TESTIMONY.[45]

It was a fine tribute – but perhaps not as fine as that of the many American soldiers who came upon Botetourt's statue during the Revolution, read the inscription, and chose to leave it unharmed.

Col. Bland's was the official, governmental response to the passing of Lord Botetourt. It was left to planter Landon Carter, writing in his journal for October 15, 1768, to appropriate his soul for Virginia:

> Yesterday came a letter endorsed from Colo. Tayloe with the death of Ld. Botetourt, our Governour, who left us the 13th in the morning. A melancholly piece of news. A fine Gentleman is dead and truly Noble in his Public character. He, as anecdote says, was pitch'd upon to be the Agent of a dirty tyrannic Ministry; but his virtues resisted such an employment and he became the instrument of a dawning happiness; and had he lived we should have been so: for through his active and exemplary virtue, order everywhere revived out of that confusion that our own dissipative indolence had thrown us into.[46]

It was perhaps as close as anyone was to come to describing Botetourt's greatness as a governor. Here on the one hand was a great lord – and statesman – who mixed good judgment with affability. Here on the other was a governor who sensed Virginians' need for order and moral certainty and supplied it instantly.

The reactions to Lord Botetourt's death by those who knew him best, his sister, the Dowager Duchess, his nephew and former ward, the Duke of Beaufort and his long time butler William Marshman, are painful to read even now, so deep and so helpless does their grief seem. In keeping with the dignity of the occasion, the Duke expressed himself in fine style. But if a surviving draft of his letter to William Nelson is any evidence, the dignity was hard won – achieved at the cost of many revisions, as the author sought emotional distance from his great loss.[47] The Dowager Duchess, who received the news in a letter from the Duke, implored him to record everything Marshman had told him about Lord Botetourt's "last precious moments . . . every syllable . . . every action, every word." "[W]ith weeping Eyes and an aching Heart," she had read and re-read the Duke's letter. Even now, she could "hardly see to write."[48] Marshman himself (who had not left Botetourt's bedside for more than half an hour in three weeks) was so "sorely grieved and dejected" by his master's tender and affectionate last words to him that he lacked the power even to repeat them.[49]

> I can justly say, without flattering his memory in the least, that while I had the honour to serve him, I never knew him guilty of a vice, but had daily and hourly proofs of his humanity and benevolence to all mankind: such instances as I shall give you of 'em when we meet, will astonish you; and I doubt not but you will join with me in thinking my present condition very unhappy and my loss irreparable.

When the time came to assign blame for Britain's loss of Virginia, most Virginians were in agreement with Richard Henry Lee in attributing it to Botetourt's successor, Lord Dunmore. "If Administration had searched thro the world for a person the best fitted to . . . procure union and success for these Colonies [he said] they could not have found a more complete Agent than . . . Dunmore."[50] But what was so right about Lord Botetourt was not necessarily what was wrong with Dunmore. Easy though it might be to cherish the memory of Botetourt after the gaucheries of his successor, how the two men were viewed depended more on how each figured in the unfolding tale of British tyranny. So it happened that the fine graces of

Norborne Berkeley seemed to shine by comparison with the vices of John Murray, and the happiness of the Botetourt years appeared more magical in the wake of Dunmore's supposed burning of Norfolk.

It would be said that Botetourt flattered Virginia egos and gained respect for English institutions. But what closed the deal was the man's unique ability to fashion order out of respect for himself. Horace Walpole's prediction turned out to be quite wrong. Lord Botetourt did not infuriate the Virginians. He charmed, fascinated and ultimately captivated them with his fine graces. Indeed, as Edmund Randolph later put it, were it not for his Lordship's "pure character," he might have thought he had been sent to Virginia "to inveigle the docility and beguile the credulity" of its people.[51]

In fact, Botetourt was an inveigler both by both nature and design, as shrewd in managing the irritable Virginians as he was deft in beguiling friends and relatives. The following letter, written by Botetourt to the Duke of Beaufort in December of 1769, suggests that the skills he used in Virginia were the result of calculation and constant practice:

> My Dear Son:
> I rejoice in your account of the Duchess – and exceedingly enjoy the idea of her meeting the sweet little Boys* at Badminton – Am much pleased with the stile in which you and your friends opposed the factious gentlemen of Gloucestershire. There is no standing that laughing good humour with which you resisted them but give me leave to complain that having sent you two speeches from hence, no return has been made to me of yours from the Bell. Lord Berkeley's neutrality was a shabby proceeding.

*The Duke's sons.

Rejoice that Mr. Southall did well and that you attended and found the Hospital in good order. Upon you and Dr. Talbot I chiefly depend for preserving and improving that great work.

The College of William and Mary is my present object. I constantly attend their morning prayers at seven o'clock and never miss evening Service unless when I am kept at home by Dining Companies. The boys seem pleased with my attention, and promise to do their utmost to crown my Labors with success. We have many plans of reform under consideration, will send them to you when they are resolved, that you may convert to the use of the sweet little men any part you shall approve.

Am much pleased with the kind manner in which you have mentioned my Sister's Determination for France. Her satisfaction in that Country will greatly depend upon the exactness of your remittances and warmth of your letters. Am sure you will pardon me for proposing that Mr. Conway may be directed regularly to transmit at a certain minute the whole you have agreed to pay her, as by that plan all possibility of mistake will be prevented.

I heartily wish that you may obtain the Lieutenancies you desire, but should you fail, shall hope I be enabled to congratulate upon your bearing well the Disappointment. The manner in which I gave up [the Lord Lieutenancy] of Gloucestershire did me more good than the holding it to the day of my death could possibly have effected.

Botetourt's gold medal
for Academic
Excellence
"The medal must go
on though it was to cost
double the money"

* * *

75

No ill humor followed the late Dissolution of the General Assembly. We met in November upon the very best terms and parted the 21st of December full of confidence in each other. I have had an admirable letter from Dr. Barton. The Medal[52] must go on though it was to cost double the money he expects it will, and so I have told him by this ship. Embrace for me the Duchess, the sweet little Boys, Mrs. and Miss Boscawen and believe me,

> Most Affectionately Yrs.,
> Botetourt

December 28th 1769

Should you find Miss Boscawen offended by the humble tender I have desired you make from me, must beg you to repair the affront by two kisses directly from yourself.

Entreat you to say to my most respectable friend Lord Berkeley of Stratton, that I have received his last kind letter, that it shall be my object to imitate his virtues and to keep in grateful remembrance the eager part he took towards obtaining for me the happy independence I now enjoy; that I shall forever love, honor and esteem him, but that for his sake I mean never to write him more – That he may perfectly understand me, you may read to him my words. Must beg that for the future you remember to tell me the dates of the letters you shall receive from hence.[53]

Botetourt's letter to the Duke contains passages of advice that, but for the author's cheery tone and irrepressible certainty of their being for the recipient's own good, might well have been taken badly. Thus, his pleasure at the Duke's mention of his mother's move to Nice turns out to be merely an excuse to remind the Duke that her future happiness will depend on regular remittances from him. Similarly, Botetourt's hearty wish that Beaufort will get the Lieutenancies is immediately followed by advance congratulations for bearing his disappointment should he fail. It is all done with the same laughing good humor that so entranced Ann Blair, except that here bonhomie runs interference for otherwise offensive meddling and presumptious advice.

In many ways, Botetourt's apologetic postscript is as calculating as the letter itself. His request that the Duke give Miss Boscawen two kisses, one for himself and one for the Duke, deftly interposes fondness for neglect while affirming Botetourt's role as the master of all ceremonies. His belated apology for not writing the aged Lord Berkeley to thank him for the Governor's job makes a virtue of a breach of good manners by sparing the Duke the effort of a reply.[54] (Afraid the old man will not get the point, Botetourt insists that Beaufort read his letter out loud – a request fully in keeping with the controlling, self-conscious personality that conceived it.) A genuinely kind man, Botetourt never fails to make the most of his kindness.

It is of course true that the letter to the young Duke of Beaufort is a special case. As his former guardian, Botetourt could speak to the Duke in a way he could not to, say, Petton Randolph. That said, the letter is in the same suavely presumptuous style of all of Lord Botetourt's discourse. In contrast with the deeply-conflicted Fauquier, Norborne Berkeley knows exactly what he wants, whether it has to do with putting down an uprising against the practice of inoculation, manipulating his nephew or making sure that a kindly old man goes away feeling more loved for being neglected. To modern readers, reared on barefaced lies masquerading as "spin," Botetourt's strategies for anticipating and controlling the reactions of his audience may seem obvious, perhaps even offensive. But that is not how they were taken; nor would that be a fair description of Botetourt's artfulness. In expressing himself in the strongest manner, in rejoicing exceedingly with endearments, Lord Botetourt dominated the space in and outside his letters, causing others to *want* to do his will. It was a style as suited to the fond uncle and militia colonel as it was to the governor of Virginia, so deft that it could wryly attribute the calm of a fractious assembly to the severity of the season even as it called down a perfect deluge of "utmost kindnesses" to reassure a concerned sister. The letter, dated December 18,1770, is one of Botetourt's last letters to his sister, the Dowager Duchess: "The Assembly of Virginia are still sitting, but from the severity of the season I expect every hour to be desired to give them leave to adjourn over the Christmas Holidays and not to meet again till the month of May. They have acted a most becoming part by the Crown and have treated me in every instance with the utmost kindness and regard. What the womb of time may produce no one can say, but it is with great satisfaction I can assure you that I have at present the fairest prospect of being able to do some good in this distracted age. May the Almighty realize my expectations."[55]

In *The Creation of the American Republic*, Gordon Wood notes that "Americans were not an oppressed people; they had no crushing imperial shackles to throw off"[56] – to which we might add that no one in America was less oppressed or more alert to occulted signs of tyranny than a white Virginia planter. What makes the Revolution in Virginia so interesting is what makes it so boring: the lack of good causes for rebellion. There was no Norfolk Port Bill; no Williamsburg massacre. There were no British "lobsterbacks" in the streets; no pall of gun smoke over Market Square. We can see at a glance that Virginia was not Boston. It was the most *British* colony in America. In the ten years from Patrick Henry's call for a Cromwell to stand up for his country against George III to his "Give me liberty or give me death!" speech in Richmond's First Episcopal Church, Virginians' respect for what many viewed as a "beloved British constitution" never ceased. Life went on pretty much as usual, despite occasional efforts to get up a boycott of English goods. Much of the impact of Parliament's punitive laws fell where it was intended to fall: on Boston. One of the reasons that radicals like Arthur Lee were so preoccupied with the notion of a British plot to "*sap*, not to *storm* [America's] freedoms" was because there was so little evidence of it in Virginia.[57]

Norborne Berkeley was a great governor, not because he had fine manners, or because he was so deft in manipulating the overactive egos of Virginians. He was great because he stayed in character; because he took pleasure in finding people doing something right, and when he caught them doing something wrong, he let them know it promptly, firmly and clearly. He showed Virginians that he valued them even as he gave them reason to value his good opinion. The bond between Botetourt and the people of Virginia was forged, like the man himself, from iron.

Had Lord Botetourt not died and there been no Earl of Dunmore to provide them with an excuse, Virginians would have rebelled anyway, as theirs was a revolution that required no cause. Colonial Virginia was not in need of independence so much as it was in need of emotional release. Lord Botetourt's 1769 speech to the House of Burgesses pledging to hold the government to its promise to lay no further revenue taxes on America was a fine, if ultimately futile gesture, so shocking to Hillsborough that he rebuked Botetourt for saying exactly what he had been instructed to say, so implausibly alien to Edmund Randolph that he actually rejoiced at Botetourt's "timely death."[58] Thomas Jefferson evidently shared

Randolph's sense of relief. As he told Daniel Webster in 1824,

> Lord Botetourt was an honorable man. His government
> had authorized him to make certain assurances to the peo-
> ple, which he made accordingly. He wrote to the minister
> [Lord Hillsborough] that he had made these assurances,
> and that, unless he should be enabled to fulfill them he
> must retire from his situation. This letter he sent
> unsealed to Peyton Randolph for his inspection. Lord
> Botetourt's great respectability, his character for integrity,
> and his general popularity, would have enabled him to
> embarrass the patriots exceedingly. His death, therefore,
> was a fortunate event for the cause of the Revolution.[59]

There is no letter of resignation from Lord Botetourt in the
surviving files of the Board of Trade – which is not to say it was
not sent, not all letters from colonial governors having made it
to London or into ministry files. Instead, we find this sentence,
surely the most elaborately sarcastic ever penned by a royal
governor: "Upon my Knees I ask pardon of the King, if I have
been improper in declaring to his People my Sentiments of His
Majesty's Aversion to the arts of Deceit."[60]

In the end, not even the sarcasm of Lord Botetourt could
save Virginia for England. It was not the government's failure to
redress their grievances that pushed Virginians over the edge.
They were already feeling empowered – "prodigious in spirit,"
as John Adams would later put it.[61] Rather, it was the failure to
recognize the claims of Virginia planters to exceptional status.
The paradox that Edmund Morgan and other historians have
found so troubling, of haughty Virginia "slaveholders devoting
themselves to freedom," stands: Virginians' ideas of tyranny
were not at odds with the nature of their society but a reflection
of it; not a rejection of slavery but its mirror image.

Lord Botetourt as he looked when Governor of Virginia

Notes

1 Jack P. Greene, ed., *The Diary of Colonel Landon Carter of Sabine Hall,* 1752–1778 (2 vols.; Charlottesville, 1987) 1: 512.
2 Quoted in Graham Hood, *The Governor's Palace in Williamsburg* (Williamsburg, 1991) p. 275.
3 The description of Lord Dunmore as a reputed gamester, whoremaster and drunkard can be found in a letter from James Parker to Charles Steuart, 19 Apr. 1771, as quoted in Hood, *The Governor's Palace,* p. 280.
4 *Virginia Gazette* (Dixon & Hunter), 5 Aug. 1775.
5 Horace Walpole to The Hon. Henry Seymour Conway, 9 Aug. 1768, in Peter Cunningham, ed., *The Letters of Horace Walpole* (9 vols.; Edinburgh, 1906), 5: 116.
6 See *Virginia Gazette* (Rind), 10 Mar. 1768. The suspicion of partiality was founded partly on Fauquier's own words and partly on his conduct.
7 See the essay on Fauquier at the front of this volume for a more complete discussion of this issue.
8 George Mercer to James Mercer, 16 Aug. 1768, George Mercer, *Letters to his Brother, (James Mercer),* 1768 *and* 1771, Mercer-Garnet Papers, Library of Virginia, Richmond.
9 *Ibid.*
10 Horace Walpole to The Hon. Henry Seymour Conway, 9 Aug 1768, in Cunningham, ed., *The Letters of Horace Walpole,* 5: 16.
11 *Ibid.*
12 On the "Magnate of Gloucestershire," see Bryan Little, "Norborne Berkeley, Gloucester Magnate," *Virginia Magazine of History and Biography,* [1955] 63: 380.
13 Norborne Berkeley to Lord Hillsborough, 9 Oct. 1768 in Dianne J. McGaan, ed., "The Official Letters of Norborne Berkeley, Baron de Botetourt, Governor of Virginia, 1768 – 1770," (M.A. thesis, College of William and Mary, 1971), p. 37.
14 Undated, unsigned letter, not in Botetourt's own hand but clearly dic-

tated by him, beginning, "I anchored in Hampton Roads, Tuesday, 25th of October . . . ," (hereafter, "undated, unsigned letter"), Personal Collection of His Grace the Duke of Beaufort, Badminton, Gloucestershire (hereafter "Badminton Papers.") The letter appears to be a draft of Botetourt's official report to Lord Hillsborough dated November 1, 1768. See Norborne Berkeley to Lord Hillsborough, 1 Nov. 1768, McGaan, ed., "The Official Letters of Norborne Berkeley," pp. 37–39.

15 George III to Lord North, 27 Mar. 1782, Sir John Fortescue, ed., *The Correspondence of King George the Third from 1760 to December 1783*, (6 vols.; London 1927-28), 5: 418

16 "Additional Instructions for Our Right Trusty and Well beloved Norborne Barron DeBotetourt," 21 Aug. 1768, Colonial Williamsburg Foundation (microfilm).

17 Undated, unsigned letter, Badminton Papers.

18 Judge St George Tucker to William Wirt, 25 Sept. 1815, *William and Mary College Quarterly*, (1913–14), 22: 252. After his death in the fall of 1770, Botetourt's state carriage was given to the colony by the 5th Duke of Beaufort. It was still there in 1781, where it was described (with obvious distaste) by Timothy Pickering, a dour New Englander: "In a building near the palace are to be seen the remains of the richly-ornamented *state coach*, which was brought over with Lord Botetourt, and once used by him to carry him from the palace to the Capitol. 'Tis a clumsy machine, and enormously heavy – perhaps equal to two common wagons. It is gilded in every part, even the edges of the tires of the wheels. The arms of Virginia are painted on every side. The motto of the arms led me to remark how peculiarly disposed the Virginians have been to adopt ideas of royalty and magnificence . . . .The motto is, *En dat Virginia quartam*, – that is, 'Virginia gives a fourth quarter to the world.'" Octavius Pickering, *The Life of Timothy Pickering* (4 vols.; Boston, 1867), 1: 297–298.

19 "*From an* English *Paper of* October 10th, *To the* PRINTER,"*Virginia Gazette* (Purdie & Dixon), 12 Jan. 1769 (the letter is signed "One of the Community").

20 *Virginia Gazette* (Rind), 3 Nov. 1768.

21 *Ibid.*

22 *Virginia Gazette* (Purdie & Dixon), 27 Oct 1768.

23 Horace Walpole to Richard Bentley, 24 Dec. 1754, Cunningham, ed., *The Letters of Horace Walpole*, 3:275. The term "boncoeur" was meant to

rhyme with Botetourt's name – one more reason to believe (if any more were needed) that the usual pronunciation "baht-a-taht" is dead wrong.

24 Robert Carter Nicholas to Arthur Lee, 1 May 1769, *Lee Family Papers, 1742–1795*, University of Virginia microfilm.

25 Arthur Lee to Richard Henry Lee, 15 Nov. 1769, *Lee Family Papers*.

26 Ann Blair to Mrs. Mary Braxton, 21 Aug. 1769, *Blair, Banister, Braxton, Horner and Whiting Papers, 1760 – 1890, 1765 –1817*, Manuscripts and Rare Books Department, Swem Library, College of William and Mary.

27 Robert Jackson to his sister, 15 Sept. 1759 and 12 Jan.1760, quoted in Little, "Norborne Berkeley," 63: pp. 390–91.

28 *Ibid.*, 63:396.

29 Will of Francis Fauquier, in Hood, *The Governor's Palace*, p. 228.

30 *Virginia Gazette* (Purdie & Dixon) 18 May 1769.

31 Botetourt to Lord Hillsborough, 19 May 1769, McGaan, ed., "The Official Letters of Norborne Berkeley," pp. 135–136.

32 James Parker to Charles Steuart, 20 Oct. 1769, *Charles Steuart Papers* (MS 5025, f. 215), National Library of Scotland. Of this incident, John Page, Jr., wrote in May 1769 "this [dismissal] has not lessen'd him in [the burgesses'] Esteem, for they suppose he was obliged to do so; he is universally esteemed here, for his great Assiduity in his Office, Condescension, good Nature and true Politeness." John Page, Jr., to John Norton, 27 May 1769, Frances Norton Mason, ed. *John Norton & Sons, Merchants of London and Virginia*, (Richmond, 1937), p. 94. The similarities between the leadership styles of Botetourt and Washington are remarkable.

33 Charles Bragge to Norborne Berkeley, 2 Feb. 1767, quoted in Little, "Norborne Berkeley," 63:406.

34 Robert Carter Nicholas to Arthur Lee, 29 Dec. 1769, *Lee Family Papers*.

35 James Parker to Charles Steuart, 20 Oct. 1769, *Charles Steuart Papers*, (MS 5025, f. 215).

36 James Parker to Charles Steuart, 6 May 1769, quoted in Frank L. Dewey, *Thomas Jefferson, Lawyer* (Charlottesville, Va. 1986) pp. 48–49.

37 Greene, ed., *Diary of Colonel Landon Carter*, 1: 512.

38 Robert Carter Nicholas to Arthur Lee, 29 Dec. 1769, *Lee Family Papers*.

39 James Parker to Charles Steuart, Dec 1770, quoted in Hood, *The Governor's Palace*, p. 208–209.

40 *Virginia Gazette* (Purdie & Dixon), 18 Oct. 1770, Supp. See the October 15, 1768 diary entry of Landon Carter, *infra*, for a description capturing

some of the epochal significance of Botetourt's passing.

41 *Ibid.*

42 William Nelson to the Duke of Beaufort, 30 Oct. 1770, Badminton Papers.

43 Duke of Beaufort to William Nelson, 1 Jan. 1771, Badminton Papers.

44 John Pendleton Kennedy, ed., *Journals of the House of Burgesses, 1770–1772* (Richmond, 1906; facsimile reprint, Bowie, Md. 1996), pp. 122, 138.

45 Quoted in Hood, *The Governor's Palace*, p. 275.

46 Greene, ed., *Diary of Colonel Landon Carter*, 1: 512.

47 See undated, unsigned draft of letter from the Duke of Beaufort to William Nelson, 1 Jan. 1771, Badminton Papers.

48 Dowager Duchess of Beaufort to the Duke of Beaufort, 30 Jan. 1771, Badminton Papers.

49 William Marshman to John Marshman, 8 Nov. 1770, Badminton Papers.

50 Richard Henry Lee to Mrs. Catherine Macaulay, 29 Nov. 1775, James Curtis Ballagh, ed., *The Letters of Richard Henry Lee*, (2 vols.; New York 1911-1914) 1: 162.

51 Edmund Randolph, *History of Virginia*, Arthur H. Shaffer, ed. (Charlottesville, VA 1970) p.170.

52 That is, the gold medals that were to be awarded to William and Mary students. Dr. Barton, who was apparently acting as Botetourt's agent in this matter, has not been traced.

53 Norborne Berkeley to the Duke of Beaufort, 28 Dec. 1769, Badminton Papers. The 5th Duke of Beaufort (1744-1803) married Elizabeth Boscawen in 1766. By the date of this letter, they had had two sons – Henry, born 1766, and Charles, born 1767.

54 The shaky handwriting of Lord Berkeley of Stratton's letter to Botetourt congratulating him on his appointment testifies to Botetourt's wisdom in sparing the old man further efforts of that sort. See Lord Berkeley of Stratton to Norborne Berkeley, 1 Aug. 1768, Badminton Papers.

55 Norborne Berkeley to the Dowager Duchess of Beaufort, 18 Dec. 1769, Badminton Papers.

56 Gordon Wood, *The Creation of the American Republic 1776–1787*, (Chapel Hill, 1969), p.3

57 Arthur Lee, "Monitor I," *The Farmer's and Monitor's Letters to the Inhabitants of the British Colonies*, (Williamsburg, 1769; reprint, 1969), p.61

(Italics in Original).

58 Botetourt's speech can be found at *Virginia Gazette* (Rind), 9 Nov. 1769. In *History of Virginia*, Edmund Randolph, expressed grave doubt whether, if push had come to shove, Botetourt would have "renounced ... every tie to the mother country and ... become an exile to England among a people to him, as it were, alien." "Human nature forbids such expectations," Randolph went on to say, "I rejoice therefore that he died so timely," thereby expressing his strong preference for a history untainted by the unaccountable integrity of a man "to whose ear the term omnipotence, as applied to this country, conveyed neither ... blasphemy nor a suspicion of credulity." Randolph was apparently unaware of Boteourt's scathing reply and Hillsborough's reprimand. Randolph, *History of Virginia*, pp. 172–173.

59 Fletcher Webster, ed., *The Private Correspondence of Daniel Webster*, (2 vols; Boston, 1857; reprint, University of Michigan University Library), p. 369.

60 Norborne Berkeley to Lord Hillsborough, 14 Apr. 1770 (acknowledging his receipt of Hillsborough's "Reprehension . . . in No. 29"), McGaan, ed., "The Official Letters of Norborne Berkeley," p. 217a. It is perhaps worth noting that virtually every technique used by Botetourt can be found in the well known management primer, *One Minute Manager* – from his "One Minute Praising" of the crew and officers of the *Rippon* ("catching people doing something right") to his scathing (but brief) "One Minute Reprimand" of William Nelson at the conclusion of the trial of Cornelius Calvert and Dr. Dalgleish. Ken Blanchard and Spencer Johnson, *The One Minute Manager* (New York, 1982), p. 92.

61 John Adams Diary, entry for 23 Aug. 1774, in L.H. Butterfield, ed., *Diary and Autobiography of John Adams* (4 vols., Cambridge, Mass., 1961), 2:109.

62 Edmund S. Morgan, *American Slavery, American Freedom* (New York, 1975), p. 4.

A Few Words on Virginia Slavery and the Revolution

This is a series about a battle with irony as fierce as the Revolutionary War itself. It is also a series about the overwrought narratives Virginians fashioned to avert those ironies. Some of the Virginians' narratives – those in their letters, for example – were ostensibly private. Others, like Patrick Henry's speeches, Arthur Lee's Monitor essays, George Mason's *Declaration of Rights* and Thomas Jefferson's *Summary View of the Rights of British America* and the American Declaration of Independence, bear all the marks of full-dress theatrical performances. Whether they were speaking to an audience of one or a hundred, Virginians never forgot they were addressing posterity.

Edmund Morgan has said that Revolutionary-era Americans "allowed Virginians to compose the documents that founded their republic, and they chose Virginians to chart its course."[1] That is true. But if Jefferson's Declaration of Independence put words to the visioning of America it also imported to that vision as subtext the defining fact of life in Virginia: black African slavery. Slavery is not listed among Jefferson's self-evident truths. This was after all political propaganda. But the fact is, without slavery, Jefferson would not have had the time or the leisure to imagine America.

This is not to give slavery credit as the atrocity which "sensitized" Virginians to the blessings of liberty.[2] It is however to

---

[1] Edmund Morgan, *American Slavery, American Freedom* (New York, 1975), p. 387.
[2] See Robert Middlekauff, *The Glorious Cause* (Oxford, 1982), p. 606

remind ourselves that nothing in 18th Century Virginia is conceivable without slavery. Slavery supplied white Virginians with half their net worth, nearly all of their labor and their most stressed paradox: that they were themselves English slaves.

So fiercely did white Virginians covet their liberty, so proud and powerful were they in disposing of their human property, that there seems to be no parallel for it anywhere, except perhaps in the time of Republican Rome, that golden idyll so beloved by classically-educated Virginia gentlemen. Of course, the slaves in this latter-day idyll do not have names. Literacy being power in Virginia, the mark of individual slaves on history is a frail "X." Their status as enduring metaphor is however unassailable.

One of America's best critics, Richard Poirier, has described the "extravagances of language" in American letters as "an exultation . . . of consciousness momentarily set free." "The most interesting American books," he wrote, "are an image of the creation of America itself, of the effort . . . to 'Build therefore your own world.'. . . They are bathed in the myths of American history; they carry the metaphoric burden of a great dream of freedom – of the expansion of national consciousness into the vast spaces of a continent and the absorption of those spaces into ourselves."[3] Poirier was talking about American prose fiction; in particular, 19th-Century American novels. Whether the writings of 18th-Century Virginians were bathed in the myths of history he did not say. But certainly it is hard to imagine a more compelling image of the creation of America itself than Thomas Jefferson's Declaration of Independence – or one more devoted to building its own world.

To emphatically declare the right to liberty a self-evident truth even as he was continuing to hold (in his own words) "the

3 Richard Poirier, *A World Elsewhere* (Oxford and New York, 1966), pp. 7, 3;

[slavery] wolf by the ears" not only defied belief; it made a mockery of it.[4]

Yet Virginians did more than embrace the paradoxes of Jefferson's great dream, they added to them. Having blamed the British government for bringing slavery to America, they did not hesitate to blame themselves – with equal vehemence – for having failed to rise above their own "dissipative indolence."[5]

By the time this book opens, the Virginians had been in a bad mood for years. Most grew one cash crop, tobacco, commerce in which was exclusively limited to Great Britain. Barred by law from issuing their own currency and obliged to pay excessive prices for the latest fashions, they were incensed to find darned holes in their "new" stockings just arrived from London. They liked to say "an English pronunciation is best," but found English condescension intolerable. They hated "dependency"; but given the chance would gladly accept appointment to a crown office. Virginia society was not like that of the other colonies. It was more proud; it was also more English. Virginians were not like other Americans. They were "prodigious in spirit" – even the Bostonians said that.

"Prodigious in spirit", "the most spirited and consistent of any" – one delegate to the First Continental Congress called the Bostonians "mere milksops" compared to the Virginians.[6] First impressions are made to be changed of course and what was once said of all the delegates from Virginia, even the most

4   Thomas Jefferson to John Holmes, 24 Apr. 1820, *The Thomas Jefferson Papers Series 1. General Correspondence, 1651–1827*, http://hdl.loc.gov/loc.mss/mtj. mtjbib023795.

5   *The Diary of Colonel Landon Carter*, Jack P. Greene, ed. (2 vols., Richmond, 1987), 1: 512.

6   Quoted in George Morgan, *The True Patrick Henry* (J.B. Lippincott and Co., 1907); reprint, American Foundation Publications, Bridgewater, Va. 2000) p.157. The delegate was Joseph Reed.

conservative, would eventually be reserved for just one: Patrick Henry, Jr. That is too bad, not because Henry was any less prodigious than legend tells, but because what made him so was his unique ability to give voice to the prodigious spirit of America. Nor is it difficult to trace the origins of this spirit to the mental and physical landscape of Virginia: the widely-dispersed, largely self-sufficient farms and plantations, each of them a virtual "little city"; the sense of near total autonomy that left the Virginia planter free to perfect his tyranny over his slaves at the very moment he was reacting with indignation to British encroachments on his own liberty.[7]

Slavery made white planters rich; but it was a wealth counted in lives which could not be spent. Slavery degraded the slave; but like all absolute power it also weakened and corrupted the master, belying his affectations of moral superiority and defeating his attempts at economic independence. Slavery was evil; and slavery supplied the Virginians with a handy metaphor for British tyranny. In short, Virginia bequeathed America a definition of liberty as deeply conflicted as Virginia itself; one which was linked, both figuratively and in fact, to a despotism far worse than any practiced by Parliament.

A subtitle for this series might be "the untold story of an unknown revolution." But any reader expecting to encounter the usual stuff of which revolutions are made – war, political and social chaos, or a French-Revolution-style reign of terror – is in for a surprise. There was no British massacre in Williamsburg, accordingly, there was no cause for vengeance; no garrisoning of British troops in Virginia houses, and thus no reason to complain of oppression; no closing of Virginia's ports, and thus no need to

---

[7] Letter of Phillip V. Fithian to John Peck, August 12, 1774, *Journal and Letters of Phillip Vickers Fithian*, ed. Hunter Dickinson Farish (Williamsburg, 1957), p. 161, 238fn1.

punish an entire population for the acts of a few. Instead of a Battle of Lexington and Concord there was a *threatened* march on Williamsburg, not by a British occupation force, but a ragtag collection of militia commanded by Patrick Henry. The first conflict of the war in Virginia was no Bunker Hill, just a sad mowing-down of British grenadiers at Great Bridge, a miserable village defended by a wretched fort called "the Hogpen." Had not Cornwallis retired to Yorktown in 1781, Virginians might have been bystanders to their own revolution.

But if Virginia's battle against tyranny seems to lack for excitement, it is not because Virginians lacked for patriotic fury. It is because their battle, enacted as it was on the stage of a slave colony, seemed so preposterous. Instead of mob action on Boston Common we have Thomas Jefferson's lifelong effort to "carefully avoid . . . every possible act or manifestation on [the] . . . subject [of slavery.]"[8]

This a series about a revolution that was destined from the start to be imperfect; about a place and a people who have yet to find their rightful place in histories of the period. Not all of these people were rebels. Not all of their actions can be described as revolutionary. The Virginians liked to argue; they liked to write even more, and often kept copies of their letters. Some of their letters now seem artful, some merely oblique and some (like those of Patrick Henry) so effortlessly transparent as to require us to imagine an audience to make them intelligible. Their value lies less in what they say than in how they enact the stressed ironies of life in Virginia. Virginians really did see themselves as actors on a stage, but it was a classic, not a Georgian stage, and they were not only the principal actors but a chorus reflecting on the meaning of their actions. To treat the Virginians' well-chosen words merely as a quarry

---

8 Thomas Jefferson to George Logan, 11 May 1805, Paul Leicester Ford, ed., *The Writings of Thomas Jefferson*, 10 vols. (New York, 1892–1899), 9: 141.

for facts would be silly. Virginians used words to aggrandize.

So what do Virginians' words tell us about them and their revolution? Among other things they tell us that for lack of good cause to rebel, Virginians seized upon a deeply unpopular royal governor, Lord Dunmore, and found in him a plausible caricature of everything they despised; that the prodigious spirit of the Virginians was both a reaction to and a predisposition for tyranny; and that if Williamsburg is the most studied 18th-Century city in the world, Virginia itself remains mostly unread.

It is not too late to put that to rights. The close reading of the letters and diaries of historical figures is not an arcane science, any more than say, the close reading of a novel. Nor must it lead to new approaches to Virginia itself, though it may challenge some old ones. This is not a history of Revolutionary Virginia, though it might qualify as a prospectus for one, being in part a meditation on a theme of neglect as revealed in the works of those historians who like to think of 18th-Century Virginia as a place far, far away; that is, anything but a slave colony. For some people, the discovery of Founder DNA in the descendants of slaves will always be a revelation.

The popularity of books like Joseph Ellis's *American Sphinx* suggests Americans are willing to reinvest in Virginia's Founders, even the fallen ones, as long as the story is well told. I hope so, as the story of Virginia and the Virginia Founders is the back story of America itself, a narrative less about a race of heroes than a few large souls laboring to transform irony into myth. My focus on those ironies should not be misunderstood. It is in fact a manifestation of my esteem.Like Gov. Francis Fauquier, who once incautiously told their lordships at the Ministry that he had "come to love these Virginians," I have found what I abhor inextricably entwined with what I most admire.

GEORGE MORROW

Acknowledgements

Dr. Samuel Johnson once said, "It is wonderful how a man will sometimes turn over half a library to make just one book." After ten years of nearly constant work on this series, I find that I have not only turned over half a library, but a good part of my life. New friends have become old ones. Some very good friends who read the essays in this series in their very earliest versions are now gone. Meanwhile, the library – I am speaking of the ever-expanding library of the internet – has only gotten larger.

It is impossible to name everyone who helped make this series, but some I must mention. There would be no series without the love, encouragement and help of my wife, Joan Morrow. But for the welcoming attitude, expert assistance and criticism of two truly fine historians of the period, Rhys Isaac and James Horn, I would still be trying to distinguish the forest from the trees. The encouragement I received from my two chief non professional readers, Joan and Terry Thomas, turned a mere collection of dates, people and events into a study of the character of Williamsburg. Other people who read one or more of the essays and made helpful comments include my 90-year-old aunt Rosemary Bauder, Paul and Joan Wernick, Richard Schumann, Michael Fincham, Ken and Judith Simmons, Fred Fey, Cary Carson, Jon Kite and Al Louer. I also wish in particular to thank Jon Kite for obtaining the French army dossier of John Skey Eustace and for translating one of Jack Eustace's overwrought pamphlets from the French. Richard Schumann ,

James Horn and Roger Hudson kindly consented to do prefaces for one of the booklets in this series. Al Louer and Paul Freiling of Colonial Williamsburg arranged for me to see Williamsburg from the roof of the Governor's Palace, a view that put time itself in perspective.

Those who are subscribers to the British quarterly, *Slightly Foxed*, described on its website as "The Real Reader's Quarterly," will recognize some similarities between the booklets in this series and that magazine. The resemblance is no accident. When I saw *Slightly Foxed* for the first time, I immediately realized that it was the perfect model, in size, material and design for what I was looking for. With that in mind, I contacted Andrew Evans at 875 Design, the English book design firm responsible for its appearance, and asked him if would be willing to take on this project. He said, "yes," and it was not long before he and I had assembled a team of people who not only seemed to know what I wanted but were able to give me something I never expected to find: new ideas on the subject matter. I especially want to thank Gail Pirkis, the publisher of *Slightly Foxed*, for recommending Roger Hudson as editor for this series. Roger is not only a highly accomplished writer in his own right, he is truly a writer's editor.

Sadly, the genial spirit who presided over the series, read and commented on virtually every booklet and guided me through its development, died while the series was still in production. I am speaking of Rhys Isaac, the Pulitzer Prize-winning author of what is still the best book ever written on late colonial Virginia, *The Transformation of Virginia*. Rhys' presence at our dinner table will be deeply missed. But he will also be missed from the profession of history, where his exuberant writing style and elegiac approach to the past daily gave the lie to the sour souls who think history is about settling scores.

As I began these Acknowledgments with a quotation from

Samuel Johnson I would like to end with one *about* Johnson. It was spoken by someone who did not know him well, but knew of him very well, William Gerard Hamilton. For me, it is Rhys Isaac's epitaph: " He has made a chasm, which not only nothing can fill up, but which nothing has a tendency to fill up. – Johnson is dead. – Let us go to the next best; – There is no nobody; – no man can be said to put you in mind of Johnson."

About the Author

GEORGE MORROW brings a lifetime of experience to bear on the characters of the people featured in this series. He has been a university instructor, lawyer, general counsel for a *Fortune* 100 company, the CEO of two major health care organizations and a management consultant. He received his academic training in textual analysis and literary theory from Rutgers and Brown Universities. He lives in Williamsburg with his wife, Joan, and two in-your-face Siamese cats, Pete and Pris.

WILLIAMSBURG IN CHARACTER

"The greatest enemy I ever had"

BENJAMIN FRANKLIN

Described as "psychotic," "insane" and "mad," Arthur Lee has long deserved a major reassessment. He gets it in this important and entertaining book, which will surprise readers with what it has to say about the man, his enemies and the character of Revolutionary-era Virginia.

Oh! Swords and Pistols To Be Sure!

Doing Justice to Arthur Lee

Williamsburg in Character No. 3

Coming April 2011

WILLIAMSBURG IN CHARACTER